It's Dangerous to Believe

ALSO BY MARY EBERSTADT

How the West Really Lost God: A New Theory of Secularization

Adam and Eve After the Pill: Paradoxes of the Sexual Revolution

The Loser Letters: A Comic Tale of Life, Death, and Atheism

Why I Turned Right: Leading Baby Boom Conservatives Chronicle Their Political Journeys (editor)

Home Alone America: The Hidden Toll of Day Care, Behavioral Drugs, and Other Parent Substitutes

It's Dangerous to Believe

RELIGIOUS FREEDOM AND ITS ENEMIES

Mary Eberstadt

HARPER

An Imprint of HarperCollins*Publishers*

HarperCollins books may be purchased for educational, business, or sales promotional use. For information, please email the Special Markets Department at SPsales@harpercollins.com.

FIRST EDITION

Library of Congress Cataloging-in-Publication Data has been applied for.

Names: Eberstadt, Mary, author.
Title: It's dangerous to believe : religious freedom and its enemies / Mary Eberstadt.
Description: FIRST EDITION. | New York : Harper, 2016. | Includes bibliographical references and index.
Identifiers: LCCN 2016016053 | ISBN 9780062454010 (hardcover : alk. paper) | ISBN 9780062471970 (audio)
Subjects: LCSH: Christianity—United States. | Christianity—United States—Public opinion. | Religious discrimination—United States. | Religious tolerance—United States. | Freedom of religion—United States. | Hostility (Psychology) | Fear—Religious aspects—Christianity.
Classification: LCC BR516 .E355 2016 | DDC 261.7/20973—dc23 LC record available at https://lccn.loc.gov/2016016053

16   17   18   19   20   DIX/RRD   10   9   8   7   6   5   4   3   2   1

In a free country, we punish men for the crimes they commit, but never for the opinions they have.

—PRESIDENT HARRY S. TRUMAN

Contents

Introduction

Among the Believers; or, Why I Wrote This Book

"Where will we go?"

The first time I heard an American Christian ask this shocking question was around three years ago.

Following a public talk in downtown Denver about religion and secularization, subjects of my last book, I was invited to dinner with a dozen or so other guests at someone's home in the Rocky Mountain foothills.[1] It was a lively, loquacious evening. Most of those present were college-educated professionals, some with advanced degrees; all happened to be practicing Catholics, and all leaned toward the conventional end of the religious spectrum. As the conversation revealed, they were also involved in various charities—beginning with our hostess, who had just started up a new program for homeless women in a blighted area of downtown.

The company was inspiring, the atmosphere festive, and the dinner talk ranged over books and theater, local and national politics, and other engaging fare. Then someone brought up the question of children, a number of whom were also present—and the barometer of merriment plummeted.

How, someone asked as she cradled her infant, could Catholic parents protect their sons and daughters from the toxic surges of today's society—especially the rising bellicosity toward believers? This anxious query quieted the table, and more questions followed. What would these children face in the future, given the rapidly growing hostility toward religious faith? In twenty years, another guest mused, would practicing Christians even be admitted to elite institutions, like Ivy League schools and prestigious companies and law firms—or denied, on account of their beliefs?

People spoke of the anti-religious fusillade now riddling popular culture via movies, books, videos, cartoons, and related popular fare that denigrates people of faith. They spoke about the ongoing vilification of Christians, especially, as "haters" and "bigots." Some asked: What is a believer to do these days? Withdraw into tiny communities, as disparate thinkers have lately urged, hoping like the monks of yesteryear to ride out a new dark age? Or should they instead stand tall as witnesses, and endure castigation in the newly virulent public square? What about other options, like moving to other states or even other countries where religious people could live out their faith in peace—and where, if anywhere, did such places exist?

Or as someone, somewhere in the mix put it, "Where will we go?"

None of us are strangers to the so-called culture wars: the long-standing, passionate, bitter debates over school prayer, abortion, pornography, sex education, same-sex marriage, transgenderism, women in combat, and the rest; or to wider, related cultural transformations, like the ascendency of the new atheism beginning a decade ago, or the accompanying rise of secularism and secularization—what the late intellectual and Catholic priest, Fr. Richard John

Neuhaus, dubbed "the naked public square."[2] Momentous though all of these developments have been, they're also no longer news.

But what's happening among Western religious believers today—the seismic shift represented by that question heard first in Denver three years ago—is like nothing that has happened before. Here were serious people so concerned that their religious faith was at risk that they were wondering whether to go somewhere else. By 2016, in many influential cultural, political, and intellectual precincts, *C* for *Christian* has become the new scarlet letter.

"Where will we go?"

In the three years since that night in Denver, I've learned that this question is being asked all over. I've heard it from Baptist ministers in Texas, for example, explaining their astonishment that they—or any other Americans—had lived to see the day when a mayor of Houston would subpoena the sermons of five Protestant ministers, to see if their words about sexuality ran afoul of a new city ordinance.[3]

"Where will we go?" has also been asked by undergraduates whose religious club, InterVarsity, one of the largest collegiate associations in the country, has lately been "derecognized," or denied the privileges allowed to other student groups, on campuses in numerous states—this, for being what one writer dubbed "the wrong kind of Christian," that is, those who believe traditional moral teaching.[4]

Homeschooled Protestant evangelical college students in upstate New York; members of the Anglican Communion in Virginia and elsewhere; Dominican friars and other clergy around the English-speaking world; faculty members and administrators at several Christian colleges and universities: a lot of people feel so culturally disenfranchised that they, too, are now wondering the same thing.

Small wonder. The ranks of other people pilloried and deprived of their own "pursuit of happiness" now grow apace: the high school football coach suspended in Washington State in 2015 for kneeling to say a prayer at the end of a game;[5] the American military chaplains who claim to have been reassigned on account of their faithfulness to traditional Christianity;[6] the small business owners working in the wedding industry at a time when vindictiveness in the name of the sexual revolution is apparently boundless;[7] the Christian staffer at a day-care center who would not address a six-year-old boy as a girl, and was fired on account of it;[8] the teacher fired in New Jersey for giving a curious student a Bible;[9] and related cases in which acting on religious conviction has been punished, at times vehemently.

Consider some other recent examples:

- In 2014, Brendan Eich, the CEO of Mozilla and creator of the JavaScript programming language, loses his job after it is revealed that he donated one thousand dollars on behalf of Proposition 8, a ballot initiative in California limiting marriage to a man and a woman (inter alia, the ballot passed in 2008 by 52 percent of the vote). A cyber-shaming war ensues, and Eich resigns.[10] Author and leading same-sex marriage advocate Andrew Sullivan writes that the episode "should disgust anyone interested in a tolerant and diverse society." Among people outside religious circles, his is a minority voice.[11]

- A thirty-three-year Catholic theology teacher in New Jersey, Patricia Jannuzzi, is fired for posting statements on her Facebook page expressing Catholic teaching about same-sex marriage.[12] This follows a social media shaming campaign called "Stop Public Hate by Teachers," whose supporters include celebrities, among them Susan Sarandon. Reviewing the facts of the case for the tradition-minded interdenominational journal *First Things*, writer Matthew J. Franck asks: "Could either of our living popes get a job in a New Jersey Catholic school?" Following several weeks of legal battles and national hostility, Jannuzzi is reinstated.[13]

- Two months before the U.S. Supreme Court hears oral arguments in the landmark marriage case of *Obergefell v. Hodges*, the *New York Times* runs what once would have been a shocking front-page story: unlike any other major case in Supreme Court history, this one could attract no blue-chip firms, and no celebrity lawyers, to argue one side of the case—i.e., against the claim that there is a constitutional right to same-sex marriage—for fear of the professional and personal consequences. Michael W. McConnell, a former federal appeals court judge and Stanford law professor, observes that "The level of sheer desire to crush dissent is pretty unprecedented."[14]

- An adjunct professor at the University of Illinois, Kenneth Howell, hired to teach a class in modern Catholic social thought, is suspended from the classroom for teaching modern Catholic thought about natural law.[15] The head of the religion department explains that his explication of Church doctrine concerning homosexuality caused accusations of "hate speech."[16]

- A Christian pastor in Atlanta renowned for his work against human trafficking, Louie Giglio, withdraws from giving the benediction at President Barack Obama's second swearing-in ceremony—the day after a progressive "watchdog" group posts a sermon from the mid-1990s in which he tells Christians to "lovingly but firmly" resist nontraditional marriage, and a social media campaign against him leads White House spokesmen to distance themselves.[17]

- A visitor to the National Gallery of Art in Washington, D.C., is ordered to remove a pro-life pin on her lapel before entering, because it is a "religious symbol."[18]

- In Massachusetts, an inner-city school district votes to sever ties with a Protestant college whose students tutor failing public school students. A committee member explains, "You have to draw the line somewhere. If the Ku Klux Klan, for example, made the best school lunch in the world, we're not going to hire them to make the school lunch."[19]

- The city of Houston issues subpoenas ordering specific pastors to turn over any sermons mentioning homosexuality, gender identity—and/or the mayor.[20]

- Catholic and other Christian adoption agencies across America are kept under legal siege that drains resources from the poor and destitute people they try to serve—for the sole reason that political adversaries oppose longstanding Judeo-Christian teaching about sex.[21]

- At the University of Texas at Austin, the police department issues a disorderly conduct citation to a street preacher after students complain that his words about STDs and sex offend them. The officer explains that it is illegal to offend the students.[22]

- An evangelical Christian fire chief in Atlanta is suspended for writing and self-publishing a book professing his Christian beliefs, among them that homosexual behavior is wrong.[23] Like others on the receiving end of the new intolerance, he expresses shock and devastation: "To actually lose my childhood-dream-come-true profession—where all of my expectations have been greatly exceeded—because of my faith is staggering. . . . The very faith that led me to pursue my career has been used to take it from me."

- A U.S. Marine in North Carolina is court-martialed, given a bad-conduct discharge, and denied military benefits because she pasted a motivational passage from Isaiah 54:17 near her office computer ("No weapons formed against me shall prosper"). According to a military judge, the quotation "could be interpreted as combative . . . [and] could easily be seen as contrary to good order and discipline."[24]

These disparate stories taken from recent headlines are examples of a toxic new force now hurtling across the United States and other advanced societies. They are part of the mounting toll of a widespread and growing effort to shame, punish, and ostracize people because of what they believe. This is moral and social change for the worse—and not only in the United States, but across the boundaries of what can still be called Western civilization.

A teacher in Great Britain is fired for praying for a sick child—which her managers define as "bullying."[25] A Christian health worker in Great Britain is disciplined for "bullying and harassment" after asking a coworker if she'd like a prayer (the coworker said yes), and giving the coworker a book about conversion to Christianity.[26] A couple in Great Britain is denied status as foster parents because they will not recant unwanted passages in the Bible.[27] A delivery driver in Great Britain loses his job for leaving a crucifix on the dashboard.[28] A preschool teacher in Great Britain is fired for refusing to read a book about same-sex parents aloud to three-year-olds.[29]

Also in Great Britain, in 2015 a preacher was sent to jail for speaking "threatening" words from the Book of Leviticus. In 2008, in Canada, the Alberta Human Rights Commission charged a former Alberta pastor with a "hate crime" for a letter he sent to a local newspaper in 2002, criticizing teaching about sexuality in the province's education system; after seven years in the legal system, the ruling was overturned in 2009.[30]

All of these and many other stories have human faces, both inside courtrooms and out. At Oxford University in 2015, I met a young scholar on the verge of a PhD who was already contributing articles to prestigious academic journals. He confided that almost no one at his college knew that he was a churchgoer, because it would hurt him professionally until he got tenure somewhere. He, too, isn't alone. Nor is his apprehension irrational. By way of example, attempts by the legal defense group Christian Concern merely to rent space for a conference at Oxford kicked up enormous controversy in 2013—exactly as other efforts to acquire a hearing for religious arguments have done on secular campuses across the Anglosphere for years now.[31]

If Christians feel threatened at home, that is nothing compared to what they discern upon looking around the world. The domestic campaign against belief looks increasingly like one front in a larger global campaign against Christians, period.

During the past few years, tragedy across the birthplace of Christianity itself has hit newly weakened Western believers with scene after horrifying scene of persecution and martyrdom—and anxiety on the part of many that their secular antagonists at home cannot be made to care. The news about what radical Islam has been doing to Christians in the Middle East and Africa—slaughtering and raping and crucifying and enslaving and driving people from their communities of two thousand years—has become an agony that their Western brothers and sisters have had to struggle to bring to public attention.

Internationally renowned veteran journalist John L. Allen Jr., author of a recent book titled *The Global War on Christians*, has laid out the wholesale murder of believers in piteous detail. One example:

> At the time of the first Gulf War in 1991, Iraq boasted a flourishing Christian population of at least 1.5 million. Today the high-end estimate of the number of Christians left is around 500,000, and many believe it could go as low as 150,000. Most of those Iraqi Christians are in exile, but a staggering number have been killed.[32]

Terrible as they are, mere numbers cannot begin to capture the suffering and depravity and historical transformations that are now facts of life in the cradle of Christianity. Jean-Clément Jeanbart, the Greek Melkite Catholic archbishop of Aleppo, Syria, reports that the terrorist group ISIS has almost wiped out Christians in that country altogether.[33] Sex slavery of women and children is rampant, verified by numerous outside authorities, including the United Nations.[34] In Mosul, Iraq, one of the oldest Christian communities in the world, almost every Christian in the city fled after ISIS offered exile or death, according to the *Washington Post*; churches across Iraq now stand empty.[35]

Efforts to make this tragedy a priority in Western nations, especially in the United States, have repeatedly ended in frustration, according to those who try, even though genocide isn't—or shouldn't be—"just" a Christian problem. As Allen notes: "Just as one didn't need to be Jewish to be concerned with the fate of [Soviet] dissidents in the 1960s and 1970s, and one didn't need to be black to feel outrage over South African apartheid in the 1980s, one doesn't have to be a Christian today to be appalled by the widespread torture and murder of Christians."[36] Writing in the *Wall Street Journal* in 2015, rabbis Abraham Cooper and Yitzchok Adlerstein made the same point. "In our view, as rabbis, any immediate admissions should focus on providing a haven for the remnants of historic Christian communities of the Middle East," they urged. "Christians in Iraq and Syria have been suffering longer than other groups, and are fleeing not just for safety but because they have been targeted for extinction."[37]

Regional Christian leaders have likewise implored the world for asylum on behalf of their brethren in the Middle East. The current and former archbishops of Canterbury have protested what the latter charges are Christians "left at the bottom of the heap."[38] The pope has called today's persecution of these believers "a form of genocide."[39] The European Parliament now also calls the horror "genocide."[40]

But where has the United States been? In March 2016, Secretary of State John Kerry at last announced what people around the globe had been importuning for years: that ISIS was indeed committing genocide against Christians in Iraq and Syria. The mystery of why this declaration took so long remains. For years, a progressive president and administration repeatedly asserted that the United States must not go out of its way to help these very people qua Christians, asserting that such would amount to a "religious test." By 2015, Nina Shea, one of the nation's leading experts on religious persecution abroad, concluded, "Whether out of indifference or by intent, the administration is abandoning the members of these religious minorities."[41]

As to the argument over a "religious test," this pseudo-objection too was refuted more than once. As Daniel Williams, author of one more new book drawing attention to this ongoing disaster (*Forsaken: The Persecution of Christians in Today's Middle East*), put it in an op-ed piece titled "Open the Door for Persecuted Iraqi Christians," "Obama need not worry that, by accepting them, he would be applying a religious test to asylum seekers. Be assured: The Islamic State beat him to it."[42]

The record of these last few years cannot help but raise the question of whether the administration would have trailed the world in acknowledging this genocide had the victims been anything *but* followers of Jesus Christ. The agonies of the Christians of the Middle East have no parallels among Western believers. They have no exact parallels anywhere in the world. But in a way that many secular men and women today may not yet understand, the atrocities and suffering of people whom the devout believe literally to be "brothers" and "sisters" weigh on the hearts and consciences of their counterparts, especially in the United States. And many of them wonder why the consciences of other people, that is, their fellow citizens who are *not* Christians, for so long appeared unmoved by the same plight. The knowledge of what is happening to their fellows, combined with the growing sense that progressives in the United States and elsewhere aren't listening because these persecuted people are Christian, is one more reason why many Western believers experience today's world as newly dark—even if their own immediate well-being and security remain luxurious by the standards of Iraq and Syria and elsewhere.

There is no moral equivalence between the violent, agonizing persecution of those believers and the "soft" persecution of men and women of faith in the advanced nations. But the fact that they are not being murdered in the streets or driven from their homes does not make what is happening to today's Western Christians all right—not by the standards of free societies, and certainly not by purported secular-progressive standards of tolerance, diversity, and freedom for all.

• • •

In short, what many Western men and women of faith feel to the marrow these days is fear.

Fear that they will lose the good opinions of their neighbors, family, and friends—because Christianity, especially, is said over and over to stand on the wrong side of history; because religious faith of that particular kind is denigrated across popular culture, and disdained as retrograde or worse in many citadels of higher learning.

Fear that Christian institutions will lose tax-exempt status and have to shut down their charitable operations. Fear that the believers will have to close those operations anyway, because of nonstop lawsuits by adversaries who don't want to pick up charitable slack themselves—but who do want to punish the believers for the existence of traditional Judeo-Christian moral teaching.

People of faith today also understand that they are being driven to the margins of what's called (ironically) polite society. They worry that their religious universities and colleges will either capitulate to the demands of this newly intolerant secularism—or refuse to break, and be stripped to the bone by legal fees instead. They apprehend, above all, that their children will suffer in the decades to come: shunned by the wider world, punished in all the better places, and intimidated out of practicing the faith passed down to them.

These are visible people living an invisible story. And there are millions of them.

It is eye-opening to spend time among the believers right now. Until practically the day before yesterday, all these Christian people were just so many ordinary Americans, living and working and socializing alongside everyone else. Now some of them believe that retreat from society itself—the so-called "Benedict Option" proposed by British moral philosopher Alasdair MacIntyre at the end of his influential 1981 book, *After Virtue*, and popularized by American traditionalist writer Rod Dreher—is the only way they will save their churches, children, and souls.[43]

Some believers have even found their way to a brand-new closet: the Christian one. Consider this inquiry from the floor in 2015, after a talk to Christopolis, an association of young Catholic professionals in Washington, D.C.: "What do you say to people who are moving from internships to paid jobs, and who might not get those paid jobs if employers think we're 'too' Christian—is it all right to hide that fact?"

One commonly hears the word *outed* now to describe a believer who's been exposed *as* a believer in one or another hostile secular environment. Or consider this formulation, from a 2016 article in the *Washington Post*: "I was a closeted Christian in the Pentagon."[44] Its author reported, "I feared how coming out as a practicing Christian would define me . . . as a relatively young person in a senior position, I needed every scrap of credibility I could claim."

A prominent Christian journalist has confided that his biggest fear in life is that his own children will grow up to hate him, because they will believe the terrible things said about the faith in public these days. He happens to be someone who spends his time on all manner of do-gooding, like riding his bike in marathons to benefit handicapped children. Both his charitable pursuits and his existential fears are common among believers these days, the yin and yang of what it can mean to be a Christian in 2016.

I've heard Catholic priests in three different countries speculate nonchalantly about going to jail in the future—because they see a day coming when they're accused of "hate crimes" just for being Catholic priests, in other words, for refusing to recant and succumb to whatever militant secularism now demands. Nor is such talk "catastrophizing" in the least, as examples of jailed preachers in Great Britain and Canada, and the experiences of those Baptist preachers in Houston, go to show.

People who haven't spent time among the believers lately might be shocked to hear how Christian leaders now talk about the future. Whether or not they have any use for organized faith themselves, most modern Western men and women likely take freedom of religion for granted. After all, that "first liberty," as it is called in the history books—as well as by Catholic bishops and others trying to protect it in recent years in the face of the onslaught that brought the likes of the Little Sisters of the Poor to the Supreme Court—is one of the foundations of our country, part of the story we tell ourselves about the character of our nation.

For more than two centuries Americans have prided themselves on their commitment to freedom of religion. Readers who lean in a more secular direction might be surprised to hear that anything has happened to shake that bedrock pledge. After all, we often hear that the United States remains a deeply religious nation. Yet in recent years that historic commitment to freedom has come under siege.

Two events explain this sudden shift. First is the passage of the Affordable Care Act, better known as Obamacare, in 2010. One of its key provisions is that employers must cover the costs of contraception—even religious institutions that hold any such cooperation to be a violation of conscience. This ideological power play is understood by those institutions to be a direct challenge to their constitutional protections. The so-called contraceptive mandate forces Christian charities to participate in the dispersal of products that Christian doctrine holds to be sinful. If that isn't a head-on collision with the principle of religious liberty, what is? Not surprisingly, the mandate has resulted in an avalanche of litigation, with more than one hundred cases of objection pending in the courts.

Secular readers also may not understand the depth of violation felt in religious quarters over this mandate of the U.S. Department of Health and Human Services (HHS). Protestants, Catholics, Mormons, Jews, and others—all of whom differ among themselves theologically about contraception itself—have been driven together as never before, united in seeing this feature of Obamacare both as dangerous precedent and as a serious challenge to religious liberty in the United States. One 2013 letter and press conference spearheaded by Russell D. Moore of the Southern Baptist Convention and William E. Lori, the Catholic archbishop of Baltimore, included a coalition so religiously diverse that the International Society for Krishna Consciousness and the Church of Scientology were among those also "standing together for religious freedom," as the open letter put it.[45]

The shock of the mandate not only drove together believers of varying faiths. It also became a crucible forging orthodox-leaning together with coreligionists generally seen as "liberal" or "left." One vivid example was "J'ACCUSE!," a passionate excoriation of the Obama administration penned in the *National Catholic Reporter* by Michael Sean Winters in 2012. He wrote:

> I come at this issue as a liberal and a Democrat and as someone who, until yesterday, generally supported the President, as someone who saw in his vision of America a greater concern for each other. . . . I defended the University of Notre Dame for honoring this man. . . . I [now] accuse you, Mr. President, of dishonoring your own vision by this shameful decision.[46]

Winters went on to charge Obama variously with "ignoring the Constitution," "risking the many achievements of political liberalism," "treating shamefully those Catholics who went out on a limb to support you"—another charge that resonated widely at the time—and above all, "betraying philosophic liberalism, which began, lest we forget, as a defense of the rights of conscience."

One might wonder what it would take to drive someone accustomed to criticizing Church small-t traditionalists to pen an essay that every one of them could have signed. The answer, again, is the HHS mandate. That act of supposedly progressive fiat, in short, accomplished the seemingly impossible: it united religious people of otherwise varying political and theological opinions around a single idea, which was that a lethal threat to religious liberty has materialized, thanks to Obamacare.

The second major development was the Supreme Court's 2015 finding in *Obergefell v. Hodges*, granting same-sex couples the right to marry under the Constitution's equal protection clause. This decision effectively marked the end of religiously based opposition to same-sex marriage and has also led to an avalanche of legal activity. That same year a Colorado baker who declined on religious principle to make a wedding cake for a same-sex couple was ruled to have illegally discriminated against them. The national debate around both issues was conducted in scorched-earth terms, with no holds barred—as the campaign against Brendan Eich amply shows. Among other fallout from the baker's and similar cases, cries of "hater" and "bigot" now echo across the land, amplified by the anonymity of the Internet and social media campaigns aimed against believers.

Yet even before the passage of Obamacare, religious leaders were responding to the newly chilled atmosphere with rhetoric that should have attracted the attention of anyone concerned with freedom in this country. The late Cardinal Francis George of Chicago famously predicted almost ten years ago, "I expect to die in bed, my successor will die in prison and his successor will die a martyr in the public square."[47] At the time, the statement struck even some believers as overly dramatic. In retrospect, it was instead one early warning sign of an increasingly apocalyptic mood among people of faith.

In November 2015, the Protestant evangelical magazine *Decision* republished an essay by Billy Graham telling American believers to "prepare for persecution."[48] American Baptist minister R. Albert Mohler Jr. observes in his 2015 book *We Cannot Be Silent: Speaking Truth to a Culture Redefining Sex, Marriage, and the Very Meaning of Right and Wrong* that "[w]e should expect horrifying harm, the decline of human flourishing, and restrictions on our message and the freedom of the Christian church" in the time to come.[49] No less an authority than Pope Francis has said that Christians are being "politely persecuted" under the guise of "modernity and progress."[50]

These warnings and others like them now echo through hearts and pulpits across the United States and beyond.

Do unbelievers, and anti-believers, and others who don't think they have a stake in this fight even know that such things are said among the believers these days? If so, do any of them care? This book has been written in the countercultural hope that there are people of conscience, including and especially secular and progressive people of conscience, who will.

For today's new intolerance not only threatens everything that drew persecuted immigrants of faith to the New World in the first place. It also menaces something else that has no purchase on the wider conversation as yet, and needs to: the lives and pursuit of happiness of millions of fellow citizens, not only in the United States but across the societies of the Western world.

Many progressive-minded Americans have absorbed the belief that they are the heirs to Voltaire and Clarence Darrow, Thomas Jefferson and Martin Luther King Jr., and other apostles of secular enlightenment. They should know that a lot of what's committed against religious believers in progressivism's name these days shares no such dignified pedigree. It smacks instead of intimidation, condescension, and vengeance.

My hope is to spur all people of goodwill, regardless of belief, who will be convinced by these pages that the pan-Western secularist witch hunt against religious fellow citizens—most of it conducted by runaway activists and ideologues—has already gone too far. Two desires have compelled the writing: first, to give heart to the people who now despair that their best days as religious believers in the societies of the West are behind them; and second, to present their case in the hope that tolerant and open-minded people, especially their secular and progressive fellow citizens, will weigh it.

It's time for fair-minded men and women who want no part of today's soft persecution, who still understand that the open society depends on "agreeing to disagree," to recognize that other people are being wronged.

It also helps to recall some of progressivism's own roots—and its sometime moral allies. Religious factions like Quakers took the lead in questioning slavery. Generations later, believers of all denominations were on the front lines of the epic fights against Jim Crow. Without Catholic priests and nuns and laity, Baptist and other Protestant preachers, and run-of-the-mill churchgoers of all hues and locales, there would have been no civil rights movement—a truth to which Rosa Parks, among other Christian leaders of that movement, has served as witness.[51] Richard John Neuhaus of *First Things*—sometimes criticized by theological progressives—was one more example of a religious leader who rose to prominence battling for the civil rights of African-Americans.[52]

It helps to remember, too, that people of the left have not always been as monolithically arranged against religion and religious belief

as some aggressive activists are today. The modern pro-life movement itself, for example, had prodigious roots in progressivism, as
a new work of history now details.[53] Common cause was made in
earlier times on other fronts, too. In the 1980s, some feminists stood
shoulder to shoulder with traditionalists in arguing that pornography was deleterious to society, and especially to women.[54] Right
and left, there was also until recently a broadly shared understanding that Judeo-Christianity was a cultural template of inescapable
value—historically, morally, aesthetically, and otherwise—including
among people who weren't card-carrying churchgoers.

"In the history of civilization," wrote the late, leading progressive Christopher Lasch, "vindictive gods give way to gods who show
mercy as well and uphold the morality of loving your enemy."[55] It's a
message of surpassing urgency today.

Beneath the individual anecdotes about what's happening to today's
believers, and propelling those stories upward in the first place, lies
a larger tale that also deserves a hearing across party and religious
lines. It's about how the United States—indeed the Western world—
has come to see its politics and laws and intellectual life and much
else shaped by the contest of two opposed, fiercely held faiths: on the
one hand, the faith of the Christian religious tradition; and on the
other, the much newer secularist faith built piece by piece for half a
century atop doctrines and commandments and precepts developed
out of the sexual revolution of the 1960s.

My hope is to excavate that deeper story one chapter at a time
by drilling down through developments aboveground, on the surface of culture—namely, the various manifestations of today's potent
new hostility against non-dissenting religiosity, and the striking determination with which those new campaigns are executed.

Today's historically unprecedented penalties for religious belief call for an explanation they have not yet been given. The faithful have been on the losing end of skirmish after skirmish for decades now—some would say centuries. Yet their adversaries nevertheless continue to treat them as practically omnipotent, and perpetually malevolent, social forces, even as one cherished cause after another—nearly all the vaunted issues of the so-called culture wars—chalks up as a loss. Why?

Other blueprints come to mind when inquisitors ascribe powers to people that they do not have: the day-care hysteria of the 1980s and 1990s, the McCarthyism of the 1950s, the witch trials in Salem, Massachusetts, in the late 1600s and those around Europe for centuries before that. Contrary to the oft-told story according to which American Christians control the cultural levers of power, the reality is that they are being pressured as never before on front after front.

Consider today's unprecedented legal and other attacks on Christian colleges, Christian associations and clubs on campuses and elsewhere, and Christian homeschooling. Or the range of tactics of intimidation, shunning, and smearing now deployed against religious traditionalists. Or another tale that hasn't been told elsewhere and that didn't even exist until recent times: the ongoing legal and public relations attacks on religious charities. What kind of motivation does it take to make attacks on other people's beneficence your cause in life?

In sum, what the ferocity of today's secularist intolerance is now doing to people of faith is a story that deserves to be heard. So does the related story of how the sexual revolution has given rise to a new secularist faith of its own whose founding principles are the primacy of pleasure and self-will. If we people of the divided Western world are ever to get out of the divisive and intolerant place we're in now—as reasonable people surely want to by now—we need first to understand how we got here.

"Where will we go?"

This book is dedicated to the men and women of faith who now agonize over that question; and to everyone else, progressive and secular people emphatically included, who can be persuaded that the traditionalists deserve a hearing, too, and that today's depredations against them have gone too far. Practicing Christians living in historically free societies shouldn't have to "go" anywhere. This is especially true in America, which either remains a place where human beings can follow their faiths without hindrance—or instead becomes some other nation altogether.

As Martin Luther King Jr. put it in his "Letter from Birmingham Jail," "Anyone who lives in the United States can never be considered an outsider." Surely the same rule applies to his fellow believers today.

It's Dangerous to Believe

1

The Roots of the
New Intolerance

Today's historic explosion of intolerance toward religious believers did not erupt out of nowhere. It has a long prehistory, and it behooves us briefly to revisit that history before exploring its newest malign manifestation.

Many historians would locate the beginnings of the story in the Enlightenment, when philosophical sceptics like Voltaire and Thomas Hobbes took on the task of challenging the truth of religious dogma, thus beginning the long process of disentangling church and state and creating new space for secular thought and expression. The contributions of science continued this process by providing a rival mechanistic view of the universe. Astronomy in the sixteenth century, physics in the seventeenth century, and natural science in the nineteenth century—particularly the publications of Charles Darwin—fueled this same project, even as the French Revolution became the bloody prototype demonstrating just how much it could take for a state to try and lay waste to a church.

The urge to delegitimize and crush belief gained new allies in

the twentieth century in the form of communist and fascist dic-
tatorships benefiting from technologies that Robespierre and the
Jacobins lacked. Not content to wait patiently for the withering away
of the churches, both Nazism in Germany and communism in the
Soviet Union and elsewhere saw religion as the largest remaining
threat to totalitarian rule, a view that largely derived from the fact
that the movements were themselves founded on rival faiths of a
kind, promising redemption—a secular heaven on earth—for their
followers. Therefore both totalitarian sects campaigned vigorously,
and with impressive results, to bring believers and their hierarchies
to heel. Historian Robert Royal of the Faith and Reason Institute
is among several scholars who have argued that the twentieth century produced more martyrs, or people suffering and dying for their
Christian faith, than any other in history.[1]

The anti-religious zeal of both ideologies was shared by other
twentieth-century movements inimical to religious belief. Noteworthy among these was the Mexican government's attempt to crush
the Church in the 1920s (among other results, inspiring the English
writer Graham Greene to pen one of his best-known works, the
1940 novel *The Power and the Glory*). In Europe during the decade
that followed, and in addition to Nazi and Soviet initiatives aimed at
stamping out religious dissent, the particularly savage persecution
of Catholics during the Spanish Civil War is judged by some historians to have been worse than any other suppression of the church in
history, including even the French Revolution.

In all, Christianity across the world exited the twentieth century
with literal casualties and figurative wounds that alone would have
put the churches at a profound historical disadvantage, even without
the piling on of other adversaries since the turn of the millennium.

In other realms, too, loss became a familiar companion to religious believers. Even in liberal democracies, the preferences of the

faithful have been consistently countermanded in a series of public arenas with adverse court decisions and other legally binding changes involving school prayer, contraception, abortion, pornography, marriage, and related subjects long addressed by religious teachings. By 2016, for example, parents in the state of Virginia debate whether they will be permitted to "opt out" of having their children forced to read sexually explicit literature in public schools. One example is Toni Morrison's novel *Beloved*, which includes scenes of bestiality, gang rape, and the graphically described murder of an infant. Far from having the power to force their own views upon the world, parents who object to making books like this mandatory reading are plainly and irrefutably acting from a position of defense, not offense.[2]

Elsewhere, on the broader cultural front, a long-standing tradition of anti-religious satire, drama, and diatribe have been advancing the secularist critique for several centuries. From Voltaire's picaresque satire *Candide*, published in 1759, to Clarence Darrow's righteous drubbing of creationist William Jennings Bryan as portrayed in 1960's *Inherit the Wind*; from *Monty Python's Life of Brian* to the musical *The Book of Mormon*; from wildly popular anti-Catholic classics like William of Orange's *Apologie* (1581) to the fraudulent *Awful Disclosures of Maria Monk* (1836), Dan Brown's *The Da Vinci Code* (2003), and Hilary Mantel's *Wolf Hall* (2009), churchgoers and their leaders have been laughingstocks in all the best places for a very long time now.[3]

In sum, religious faith has been in retreat for several centuries. It has fought back, to be sure—and it fights back still. It has also known periods of intense revival, like the waves of Great Awakening between the early eighteenth and late nineteenth centuries in the United States; and the post–World War II boom in religiosity that enveloped most nations in the Western world, on account of which Christianity still retained tremendous social and political power right through the last century.[4] But something new is in the air. The past ten years in particular have delivered epochal setbacks to men and women of faith, especially Christian faith, throughout the Western world.

Two major cultural events can be blamed for this. One of these was the Catholic priest sex scandals that erupted in 2002 and continued to unfold for several years. This moral catastrophe—dubbed by Richard John Neuhaus the "Long Lent" that many Catholics and other Christians still experience in the present tense—dealt the moral authority of the Church a crippling blow from which it has yet to recover fully even over a decade later, and even with a charismatic, maverick Pope Francis at the helm.

The second of these events was 9/11. Once upon a time, atheism was a boutique phenomenon. Even in a nation with philosophical roots in the Enlightenment, most Americans were believers of some stripe, and even today a majority profess some connection to God.

Still, every village had its atheist, usually regarded as an eccentric or crank. Perhaps the most effective of these figures was Madalyn Murray O'Hair, the founder of American Atheists and a single-minded crusader for stricter separation between church and state. O'Hair was the moving force behind the lawsuit *Murray v. Curlett*, which led to a Supreme Court ruling in 1963 (*Abington School District v. Schemp*) ending school-sponsored Bible-reading in American public schools. Another issue of pressing concern to atheists was the presence of the words "one nation under God" in the Pledge of Allegiance. Atheists also campaigned (often successfully) to remove Nativity scenes from town halls and public squares, leading to conservative claims of a secularist "war on Christmas," as the slogan has it.

For most of the decades of the "culture wars," such issues did not engage the passions of the vast majority of Americans. But after 9/11, the formerly fringe concern about the overbearing presence of religion in American life entered a new phase of aggressive militancy. In retrospect, it's not hard to understand why. Fanatical Islamicists had just flown airplanes into the World Trade Center based on their belief in violent jihad as a religious obligation, rewarded by the promise of sensual pleasures in paradise. This unspeakable act of violence, driven by beliefs most people found alien and abhorrent, gave rise to a reaction that was called "the new atheism."

Thus in the aftermath of 9/11, a wave of atheist tracts appeared corresponding to and feeding public anxiety about the perceived power of a group that had nothing to do with 9/11 but was tarred with the same brush nonetheless: American Christians. According to the new atheists, we in the United States have "our own" fanatics, namely and particularly the traditionalist followers of Jesus Christ. Some of these books, like Christopher Hitchens's bestselling *God Is Not Great*, were lively and enthusiastic exercises in Christian-baiting. (This was not Hitchens's first attack on religion. He had earlier published a book going after Mother Teresa.) Some also managed ebullient digs at other faiths—as in Richard Dawkins's description of Judaism in *The God Delusion* as "originally a tribal cult of a single fiercely unpleasant God, morbidly obsessed with sexual restrictions, with the smell of charred flesh, with his own superiority over rival gods and with the exclusiveness of his chosen desert tribe."[5]

Earlier such exercises had not been amplified by the anonymity of the Internet and social media. Thanks to both, the new vilification of religious folk proved to be popular sport, like the vilification of much else in an age of instantaneous electronic connection; and these and other polemical, sometimes inflammatory texts exploded into bestsellers.

Among the more earnest offerings were those of Sam Harris,

who made his debut with a 2004 anti-theist tract called *The End of Faith: Religion, Terror, and the Future of Reason*. He followed this up with a manifesto called *Letter to a Christian Nation*. Addressing what he believed to be a majority Christian society, Harris sounded an alarm about what he considered a "moral and intellectual emergency," namely, that "the beliefs of conservative Christians now exert extraordinary influence over our national discourse—in our courts, in our schools, and in every branch of government."[6] He added that this power across the culture was "well known."

Many other people seemed to share this anxiety about the inordinate sway of religious conviction, as the proliferation of related works indicated.

In *American Fascists: The Christian Right and the War on America*, author Chris Hedges decried a putative "core group of powerful Christian dominionists who have latched on to the despair, isolation, disconnection and fear that drives many people into these churches." He further argued that these American Christians resembled the fascist movements in Italy and Germany during the 1920s and 1930s.

In *American Theocracy: The Peril and Politics of Radical Religion, Oil, and Borrowed Money in the 21st Century*, Kevin Phillips argued similarly that "strong theocratic pressures are already visible in the Republican national coalition" and that these had "warped the Republican party and its electoral coalition, muted Democratic voices, and become a gathering threat to America's future."[7]

Also in 2006, *The Theocons: Secular America Under Siege*, by Damon Linker, formerly an editor at *First Things*, argued that secularism itself was being endangered by an "enormously influential but little-understood ideology" that he dubbed "theoconservatism." Led by Father Richard John Neuhaus and other intellectuals around *First Things*, this tiny but alarmingly powerful movement threatened to "cripple" the United States itself—even to transform the nation into "a Catholic-Christian republic." [8]

In fairness, secularist anxieties about American Christians were not wholly unmoored from reality—reality of the past, that is. For most of its history, the United States did know Christianity as a dominant force. One could see a crèche on the village green at Christmas, or the Ten Commandments in a county courthouse. Nor was that all. From George Washington to Abraham Lincoln to George W. Bush, biblical imagery informed political rhetoric from the highest office in the land on down to county clerks.

And not all the signs of Christian influence were ancient history. The 1950s, in particular, saw a nationwide religious revival of such magnitude that Will Herberg, then the country's leading sociologist of religion, could remark that the village atheist was a vanishing figure on the landscape, and that "anti-religion is virtually meaningless to most Americans today." [9] The so-called Hays Code reflected the dominance of Christian sentiment half a century ago by imposing restrictions on Hollywood films, including limits on profanity, blasphemy, and ridicule of clergy.

Later, in the 1980s and for part of the 1990s, evangelical Christians—and tradition-minded Catholics, and Mormons, and Jews—did have a place at the table in Washington, D.C. Protestant evangelical media expanded via Pat Robertson's *700 Club* and other shows on the Christian Broadcasting Network (CBN); Catholics founded their own Eternal Word Television Network (EWTN); Republican administrations made room for and encouraged the rise of influential groups like Moral Majority and Focus on the Family and others. For a while there in the 1950s, and again in the 1980s and beyond, Christians whatever their interdenominational differences had momentum on their side.

And such is exactly the point: that world is no more. From the perspective of 2016, the idea that the Christian flock now menaces and encircles secular minorities is preposterous—as antiquated as decrying fluoride in the water supply, or the hazards of motorized travel. Exactly a decade after the new atheists declared the Bible Belt to be the epicenter of American power, cultural-political reality is 180 degrees reversed.

Inherit the Wind was transgressive because it appeared at the tail end of a religious boom following World War II. Its portrayal of William Jennings Bryan as a doddering, broken man humiliated by enlightenment apostle Clarence Darrow was daring at the time. Today, when secular rationalism has become the establishment view from Silicon Valley to federal bureaucracies to no-God squads throughout the West, the landscape has been transformed.

Classic movies with religious themes like *Ben Hur*, *The Robe*, and *Quo Vadis?*, and other popular entertainments predicated on Judeo-Christianity as a shared cultural heritage were once a Hollywood staple; this genre disappeared before most people reading these words were even born. They have not been replaced. Neither have the mainstream Christian writers who spoke to mass audiences across denominations *as* Christians, including outside their own precincts—popular, enduring writers like C. S. Lewis and Evelyn Waugh and Flannery O'Connor and J. R. R. Tolkien and others whose religious beliefs were elemental to their creative efforts and literary legacies. Name one such today.

No: now it is not conventional believers who are everywhere occupying figurative drivers' seats, but rather what might be called the secularist-progressive alliance: a cultural band of like-minded people, united above all by their antipathy to the traditional Judeo-Christian moral code—including many (though not all) feminists, new atheists, advocates for same-sex marriage, rationalists, soi-disant humanists, postmodernists, militant secularists, population controllers, and other fellow ideological travelers.

These activists share an understanding that if the problem in America today has a name, "Christian" is somewhere in it. It is this new coalition—not the real or imagined traditionalist majority of years past—that is now ascendant "in our courts, in our schools, and in every branch of government," to borrow from Sam Harris, as a raft of Supreme Court decisions and other cultural transformations go to show.

Consider: the Hays Code is no more; public entertainment in all forms, whatever else might be said of it, is now a libertarian dream come true. Internet pornography is a tsunami against efforts to control it, and smartphones convey that same product into the pockets of schoolchildren. Richard John Neuhaus was known for joking of religious orthodoxy and its cultural battles, "Lose a few, lose a few." [10] In retrospect, it is a pithy epitaph for engagement of the faithful in the modern culture wars.

And politics? Here, too, conventional believers have been struggling like Sisyphus on a slippery slope throughout the last ten years and more.

From 2009–16, a progressive president missed few opportunities to castigate nonprogressive American Christians with rhetoric that would have been unthinkable had it been aimed at any other group. He called them "bitter, cling[ing] to their guns and their religion." [11] He singled them out as "less than loving"—as if he or any other president would dare to say the same of other religious groups (think "less than loving Muslims" or "less than loving Jews"). [12] Even toward the end of his presidency, in a 2015 interview with novelist Marilynne Robinson, Obama lambasted American Christians yet again, opining that "here in the United States, sometimes Christian interpretation seems to posit an 'us versus them,' and those are sometimes the loudest voices. . . . [I]t seems as if folks who take religion the most seriously sometimes are also those who are suspicious of those not like them." [13]

Meanwhile, Hillary Clinton declared in a 2015 keynote address to the "Women in the World" summit that "deep-seated cultural codes, religious beliefs and structural biases have to be changed." [14] How is that imperious decree anything *but* an assertion that politics trumps religious liberty?

The same year, Vice President Joe Biden called the leading contenders for the other party's presidential nomination "homophobes" without producing a shred of evidence for that calumny—and no one in the media objected. [15]

These atmospherics have coincided with an equally remarkable series of setbacks in the courts, including and especially the court of public opinion. Despite forty-plus years of opposition and activism against the Supreme Court's decision in *Roe v. Wade*, abortion on demand remains the law of the land. As of the age of the Internet, the idea of even objecting to obscenity, let alone prosecuting it, has become a public joke. And, of course, a series of Supreme Court decisions culminating in *Obergefell v. Hodges* in 2015 have legalized same-sex marriage.

Ten years ago, Sam Harris could declare with a straight face that Christian mores dominated American public life. Today the notion that the religious counterculture can force its decidedly minority opinions about contraception and marriage and abortion onto a nation where cohabitation, out-of-wedlock births, and divorce abound at record levels is downright absurd.

Instead, as a result of secular-progressive ascendancy not only in the United States but across Europe and elsewhere, it is now religious believers who suffer the irrational "animus" of their fellows—to invoke a phrase used by Justice Anthony Kennedy and others to condemn the beliefs about marriage held by traditionalists themselves.[16] Propelled in different ways by both the priest scandals and the fact of 9/11, a new tide of anti-religious passion has washed across the countries of the Western world that shows no sign of abating any time soon, and that may not yet even have reached its high-water mark.

In sum, the story according to which it is the Christian hand that rocks the cradle of contemporary culture resonated decades ago, not now. From a Main Street awash in pornography and raunch culture to a Wall Street where corporations outdo themselves to curry progressive favor, it's absurd for anyone to carry on as if people in the pews direct any popular cultural traffic these days at all. Doctrinally faithful Christians, Protestant and Catholic alike, are not only culturally disenfranchised. They are the only remaining minority that can be mocked and denigrated—broadly, unilaterally, and with impunity. Not to mention fired, fined, or otherwise punished for their beliefs.

As noted earlier, these believers and their opponents have been clashing by night (and day) for hundreds of years. It's also clear that during the past half century—in societies across the Western world, and on issues ranging from school prayer and public religiosity to women in combat and same-sex marriage—the faithful have mostly lost battle after battle. Why, then, are they still being attacked so vehemently? What, exactly, might be threatened by their insistence on "clinging" to their outmoded beliefs and superstitions?

Given the victories celebrated by secular progressivism, it is past time to wonder at the rationality of the continuing attack against believers on one cultural front after another. Progressive activists have a creation narrative all their own, according to which they are the forces of light, and orthodox Christians the creatures of darkness.

But if anyone needs a reality check these days, it is not the people who have been routed.

After all, traditionalist Christians (like traditionalist Jews) are a decided minority in societies of the Western world today. Christians who reject religious orthodoxy, like many of those in the Protestant mainline, or who identify themselves as "Christian" just by virtue of baptism, are more numerous; but these are not the faithful whose beliefs have made them targets.

Demographic trends for all Christians, orthodox or heterodox, show clear signs of a general decline. According to the Pew Research Center's "America's Changing Religious Landscape," a study of more than 35,000 respondents released in May 2015,

> the percentage of adults (ages 18 and older) who describe themselves as Christians has dropped by nearly eight percentage points in just seven years. . . . Over the same period, the percentage of Americans who are religiously unaffiliated—describing themselves as atheist, agnostic or "nothing in particular"—has jumped more than six points. . . . And the share of Americans who identify with non-Christian faiths also has inched up.[17]

As for 56 million unaffiliated adults in the United States, the report adds, these "nones" now outnumber both Catholics and mainline Protestants.

None of this is to say that religious decline is inevitable, let alone that religion stands "on the wrong side of history," as today's crude historicism would have it. Great awakenings and other revivals have come and gone for the past two thousand years, and no prudent observer would rule out more to come. Even in the midst of current travails, the esprit de corps of American believers is being built anew, grounded on the faith that what's happening to them is less

a permanent rout than a time of testing from which future generations will emerge stronger and more dedicated than before. Tragedy, too, has driven people back to their places of worship time and
again—9/11 darkened doorsteps with new churchgoers for months
afterward, and more momentously, as World War II was followed
by a religious boom not only in the United States, but across the
Western world.[18]

Even so, one doesn't need to posit the end of Western Christianity to grasp this much: 2016 looks very different from 1980, let alone
1950.

Adding fuel to the new intolerance is the cultural clout of today's
anti-Christian antagonists of particularly ideological apparatchiks
who use intimidation and smearing as standard tactics. In that kind
of scenario, victimization is more than just a numbers game. As the
McCarthyism of a previous era goes to show, scare tactics benefit
from a multiplier effect.

And what does this newly unleashed hunt for ideological Christian dissidents now want?

For starters, the marginalizing and penalizing of religious believers, particularly small-o orthodox Christians, on the very doorsteps
of the churches of North America and Europe and elsewhere. And
this is only a start. As stories in these pages go to show, anyone who
dares to dissent from today's ideological desiderata faces heightened
risks of public ridicule, shaming, and professional setback. That emphatically includes people who once stood on the "safe" side of the
cultural divide over the sexual revolution. For the men and women
now unwillingly caught in its sights—mostly, though not only,
Christians—the result of today's ideological juggernaut is a world
more ominous than it was before.

It is time for reasonable people of all manner of belief or unbe-
lief, from all political and cultural subdivisions, to call this merciless

thing out—just as conservatives of the 1950s and beyond called out the injustices of McCarthyism, and righteous preachers in Salem called off the witch trials more than three hundred years ago, and as other people have righted wrongs before by holding their own political and cultural ranks to higher standards of tolerance.

There is no moral high ground in putting butchers and bakers and candlestick makers in the legal dock for refusing to renounce their religion; or in stalking and threatening Christian pastors for being Christian pastors; or in denigrating social science that doesn't fit preconceived ideology about the family;[19] or in telling a flight attendant she can't wear a crucifix;[20] or in firing a teacher for giving a student a Bible;[21] or in other attempts to drive believers into cultural exile these days.

Above all, there is no mercy in slandering millions of men and women—citizens, colleagues, acquaintances, schoolmates, neighbors, and fellow members of the human family—by saying that people of religious faith "hate" certain people where they do not; or that they are "phobes" of one stripe or another, when they are not. Neither should religious believers be slurred as "theocrats" and charged with secretly trying to bring about "theocracy"—that is, of being traitors and fifth columnists in their own country, another accusation with odious historical echoes. All these kinds of slander, to speak figuratively rather than legally, have insinuated themselves into the accepted conversation of our time, with objection from practically no one.

Today's secularist fanaticism needs calling out not only for the sake of the people it maligns, and not just because it demeans the persecutors themselves. It's wrong because it makes the rest of society complicit in wrongdoing. It compromises progressivism itself. As earlier literal and ideological witch hunts should have taught by now, civilized people should not stand idly by while their coworkers, neighbors, friends, and fellow citizens are falsely accused and worse in the public square.

Those civilized people are needed now, whatever their creeds or politics or practices. They should know something that many don't yet—namely, the wrongs now being committed against believers. Like the McCarthyism of the 1950s, today's ideological stalking and punishing of Christians is going to look contemptible in history's rearview mirror—something no one will want to admit having been part of; something from which anyone now involved will want to dissociate themselves.

People of the Book(s) may have become unpopular in some circles. But popularity isn't the litmus test of free people. Tolerance is best gauged by how society treats its least popular minorities. And by that standard, America today fails the test—including by progressivism's own standards. "At the heart of liberty," as Justice Anthony Kennedy put it famously in *Planned Parenthood of Southeastern Pennsylvania v. Casey* (1992), is "the right to define one's own concept of existence, of meaning, of the universe, and of the mystery of human life."

Does that sweeping formulation still include this country's religious people—or does it not?

The message heard sotto voce here and there, and sometimes openly, is that the believers somehow have it coming—that they are simply on the receiving end of deserved payback, eye for eye and tooth for tooth, because of precepts that Christianity (like Judaism before it) has taught for two thousand years. Plenty of people with grievances real or otherwise, representing varied agendas, want to punish believers of today for the sins and imagined sins of believers yesterday.

Some would say the Church deserves payback for the sex scandals of fifteen years ago. Some would have Christians punished because the teachings against sex outside of marriage have offended and continue to offend sexual minorities. Some would say punishment is in order because churches have burned heretics, or built Renaissance palaces off the backs of peasants—or promoted motherhood, or stood against abortion and infanticide. There is no shortage of people who have been wounded, or who believe themselves to have been wounded, by sinners or others wearing the Christian label.

Even so, such lines of attack remain today's version of a historically malignant doctrine: collective guilt. Punishing believers today for crimes committed by other believers yesterday—like seeking to punish members of any other group for what a small subset of them, if any, have actually done—is logically and morally bankrupt.

Hence, for example, the infamous—and unaffiliated—Westboro Baptist Church of Kansas and its ugly ad hominem signs vilifying homosexuality (and Jews, and Catholics, and others) are trotted out repeatedly by activists trying to Christian-shame the believers, as if to suggest that they are emblematic of today's followers of Jesus Christ as a whole. Secularists who don't personally know any people of the Book may believe such falsehoods. But anyone who has spent time among the believers knows that the vast majority in the United States and Europe are nowhere near any hateful place, literally or figuratively.

Churches, religious orders, religious schools, religious charities, and other institutions across the West are filled with earnest human beings who demonize no one—and who are nonetheless treated as a newly suspect class, thanks to today's promiscuous use of guilt by association. They don't deserve it.

Understanding how we got here begins with a new paradigm about today's pursuit of the faithful by influential secularist progressives.

We are living at a time of moral panic, familiar from related outbreaks in history, only with a novel twist: this one is driven by secularist rather than religious irrationalism. Cultural changes coupled with technological ones—chiefly, the amplification made possible by social media—have empowered an anti-religious minority and enabled it to pursue and punish the believers. Belligerent secularism, not religious traditionalism, is the true heir to Puritanism today.

It is standard-bearers within the progressive-secular alliance, not religious traditionalists, who now enforce dogma on the wider society, who police cultural precincts for heretics, and who shun and shame dissenters. They are the guardians of what has become a secularist substitute faith, concerning the sexual revolution and its perceived moral imperatives. And like the Puritanism of yesteryear, today's secular version does not tolerate nonconformism. Practicing Christians who refuse to cave are on the front lines of the new intolerance today. But where men and women of faith stand now, others are already following—including people who once believed themselves to be safe because they had preemptively accommodated or silenced themselves. Their gamble has failed, as examples now show.

Contrast high-flying moral rhetoric with the earthly reality of what is being done to the churches and their community members on the ground. For example, who really stands for free speech and diversity? It is said that religious people do not. What about multifaceted legal and other attacks by progressive activists on Christian schools, Christian colleges, Christian collegiate clubs, Christian students, and Christian homeschooling? Or the targeting of religious speakers who dare try to make their case to people who think differently, on campuses and elsewhere? Today's ongoing attempts to drive believers out of the national conversation is not only inegalitarian. It thoroughly contradicts progressivism's claim to value social and intellectual diversity.

The stakes in today's scramble over the future of Western religious belief are prodigious. They affect, first, the well-being and standing and livelihoods of millions of people of faith in this world—and their families, especially their children.

Hanging in the balance is nothing less than the future of free speech and free association. As philosopher Karl Popper crucially observed in his classic critique of historicism written during World War II, the open society has always had enemies.[22] So it does today. If every town and pulpit in the Western world is to be scoured for cultural subversives, every Christian school and college penalized for secular heresy, and every charitable enterprise with a crucifix over it made a legal target: if these and other scenarios whose logic has already been set into motion come to pass, then the free societies of America, Europe, and elsewhere will fast be rendered unrecognizable.

What reasonable people are being asked to understand is that the enemies of religious freedom are the enemies of liberalism itself. We people of the fractious West today need to reach a less retaliatory place. In the end and as we shall see, it is up to those with cultural power to expend it in a more magnanimous direction.

2

Anatomy of a
Secularist Witch Hunt

"Witch-hunt": pursuit of a group of persons for their supposed
characteristics or beliefs rather than for anything they have done.
—Christina Larner, *Witchcraft and Religion*, 1984 [1]

During the 1980s and early 1990s, the United States was convulsed
by a collective panic. Across the country there were numerous cases
in which fantastical stories emanating from children in day care accused providers in various centers of sexual and other abuse. As in
Salem Village (now Danvers), Massachusetts, circa 1692, supernatural elements abounded in these stories told by children.

The day-care panic began in 1983, when a mother with a child at
McMartin Preschool near Los Angeles made a series of accusations
against operators of the center: that her son had been abused in numerous ways, that employees at the day-care center had sexual en-
counters with animals, and other amazing charges that were never
substantiated.[2] It happens she was later diagnosed and hospitalized
for paranoid schizophrenia, and died of alcohol poisoning. In the
meantime, authorities contacted other parents at the school, and

soon the allegations rained fast and furious: teachers were accused of chopping up animals, sacrificing a baby in a church, making children drink blood, flying in the air dressed like witches, and otherwise engaging in activities whose fantastical nature did not prevent four generations of the family that owned the day-care center from being arrested, and having to endure one of the most expensive trials in American history.

And just as the irreality of the case did not prevent the travails of the McMartins, neither did it prevent numerous other day-care owners around the country from being caught up in a subsequent, nationwide, irrationalist panic over Satanism and the abuse of young children.[3]

Many of the allegations resulted in initial convictions, often using standards of evidence that appear tragically paltry in retrospect. And though the ultimate verdict on the day-care scares remains debated—that is, on what it tells us about society, as opposed to restitution for its victims—events did follow the classic paradigm of witch hunting in this sense: collective fury was followed by collective remorse and repentance. Within a few years, essays and books urging a revisionist view of the day-care panic would rewrite the events into the version ubiquitously accepted today: the scare was just that, and innocent people had had their lives destroyed by it. Spearheaded by journalist Dorothy Rabinowitz, whose groundbreaking work in the *Wall Street Journal* on the injustices then afoot resulted in an influential book and eventually, a Pulitzer Prize, public opinion reversed course. Many of the unjustly accused were exonerated, and those who had unthinkingly granted reality to the charges were retroactively chastened.[4]

The fact that a Salem-esque hunt for imagined predators took place within living memory reminds us that the urge to punish supposed malefactors is perennial among human beings.

This is to say that such outbreaks *can* happen anywhere, and at the hands of prominent people; sophistication and delusion cannot always be presumed to be estranged. Pampered by a self-serving narrative according to which postmodern men and women have somehow evolved to be superior to those who came before us, many today believe that our enlightened society is immune to such damaging outbursts of ignorance, superstition, and fear. We think of similar episodes in our past like the Red Scares of the '20s and '30s and the McCarthyite panic of the '50s as being firmly in the rearview mirror—on a par with the witch trials themselves.

But this is self-delusion. Stacy Schiff, author of the latest book on the Salem trials of 1692, puts the point this way:

> We too believe in any number of things . . . that turn out not to exist. . . . We too have been known to prefer plot to truth; to deny the evidence before us in favor of the ideas behind us; to do insane things in the name of reason; to take that satisfying step from the righteous to the self-righteous.[5]

More recent history confirms that neither modernity nor postmodernity offers insurance against literal or metaphorical witch hunting. The fury in France and elsewhere in the 1890s over the forged *Protocols of the Elders of Zion*, which led to pogroms across Europe, bears a close family resemblance. So do the years of anti-Semitism under the Nazis, during which Jews were systematically isolated, stigmatized, and blamed for all manner of social ills while being credited with enormous powers that they did not possess—all with little or no objection from the society around them, and all stepping stones to what became the Holocaust.

Of course, today's religious traditionalists are not being rounded up and hanged like Jews in Germany or people accused of consorting with the devil in Salem three centuries back. Even so, the broad similarity stands: Jews, accused witches, and now religious believers in general have been marginalized, punished, and assigned extraordinary powers out of keeping with reality.

Such is why, surveying today's ideological enthusiasm for exposing and punishing the faithful, a few observers have thought to use the metaphor of "witch hunt" to describe the current scene. From ubiquitous shouts of "bigot" and "hater" aimed at people who harbor newly impermissible opinions about marriage, to the targeting of believers in workplaces, on campuses, and elsewhere, today's secularist campaign abounds with one element essential to all witch hunts: inquisitorial zeal.

The objects of today's religious witch hunt do not risk death. But they are increasingly the victims of a collective outburst of moral irrationalism aimed at singling out and punishing members of a group who hold increasingly unpopular beliefs, in the name of rendering society a "safer" place. Some of them are shunned. Others risk losing their jobs, or face social penalties for their beliefs. All are at risk of ignominy should they be unlucky enough to attract the attention of today's neo-puritan enforcers.

Like yesterday's Puritans, today's neo-puritans fight similarly to defend an orthodoxy—a new and powerful *secularist* orthodoxy, according to which dissent from progressive dogma about the sexual revolution menaces society, and deserves punishment. Under this new dispensation, "bigot" and "hater" are the new "wizard" and "witch"; moreover, thanks to their talismanic power, some believers are just beginning to enter the stocks, both literally and figuratively. Let us count up some historical parallels one by one.

To call this singular development "ironic" is to understate the case. For starters, it was the progressive-minded author Arthur Miller, via his 1953 play, *The Crucible*, who did most to make the case that modern, secular people can be as prone to witch hunting as their religious forebears.[6] Yet while the accuracy of his rendition of the Red Scare may be subject to debate, the playwright's fundamental insight remains a touchstone for understanding 2016: it does not take an established church to ignite widespread unreason and unsubstantiated charges of communal betrayal. All that's needed is an orthodoxy against which perceived betrayal can be measured and defined.

Now apply that insight to the present. For more than half a century now, at least since the invention of the birth control pill, men and women of the West, especially secularists and progressives, have collectively assembled just such an orthodoxy, thinkingly or no. In place of the Judeo-Christianity of yesterday, and mimicking its outlines to an uncanny degree, this new body of belief has by now a well-developed secular catechism. Its fundamental faith is that the sexual revolution, that is, the gradual destigmatization of all forms of consenting nonmarital sex, has been a boon to all humanity.[7]

The fundamental principle and starting point of the new secular morality is that freedom may be defined as self-will. "Doing what you want" is the new master ethic.

The first corollary to this axiom is that pleasure is the greatest good. "If it feels good, do it" was the battle cry of the sexual revolution.

It follows from this self-evident truth that traditional moral codes represent systems of unjust repression. In the new dispensation, traditional restrictions and attitudes are viewed as judgmental, moralistic—even as forms of socially sanctioned aggression, especially against women and sexual minorities. In this profound and still-unfolding transvaluation, yesterday's "sinners" have become the new secular saints; and yesterday's "sins" have become virtues, as positive expressions of freedom.

Hence the first commandment of the new secularist writ is that no sexual act between consenting adults is wrong—possibly excepting cases of adultery. This aspect of developing doctrine, along with a few others, is not yet settled. As a historical matter, there has been catechetical confusion about this last point at least since the invention of the Pill—from sometime endorsements of "swinging" in the 1960s and 1970s, to today's new trial balloons for polygamy, such as Politico's "It's Time to Legalize Polygamy," Slate's "Legalize Polygamy!," the shows Big Love and Sister Wives, and related what-ifs. Witness too the recent use of the word monogamish to describe an altered understanding of marriage.[8]

Also consistent with a body of thought that is still evolving, there is new thinking about zoophilia. Princeton philosopher Peter Singer and others applying the optic of utilitarianism to sexual ethics have argued against the Judeo-Christian condemnation of having sex with animals. Other trial balloons for this practice, too, have been loosed of late, including in some high-profile places like New York magazine: because if consenting sex is always and everywhere a good, and if animals can be argued successfully to have given consent (which is always the ethical point on which the argument turns), then there is obviously no reason in principle to object to zoophilia.[10]

Despite these and other quasi-theological detours, which after all amount to a minority of what's under general discussion, the founding faith of contemporary secularist-progressivism is plain enough. It is that sex between consenting adults is good—and since sex is good, the more sex, at least in theory, the better.

Two corollary imperatives are that whatever contributes to consenting sexual acts is an absolute good, and that anything interfering, or threatening to interfere, with them is ipso facto wrong.

Note the absolutist character of these beliefs as they play out in practice. For example, it is precisely the sacrosanct, nonnegotiable status assigned to contraception and abortion that explains why—despite historical protestations of wanting abortion to be "safe, legal, and rare"—in practice, secularist progressivism defends each and every act of abortion tenaciously, each and every time.

For example, this new faith will not even draw the line at what is known as "partial-birth" abortion, a procedure during which, as the late surgeon general C. Everett Koop described, "a doctor pulls out the baby's feet first, until the baby's head is lodged in the birth canal. Then, the doctor forces scissors through the base of the baby's skull, and crushes the skull to make extraction easier."[11] Partial-birth abortion is such that even the late senator Daniel Patrick Moynihan, a liberal who was no ally of traditionalists, once called it "close to infanticide." Yet even partial-birth abortion does not sway the conviction of activists who defend it.

If abortion were truly an exercise of "choice"—if the rhetoric of the people who defend abortion matched the reality of what they actually, in practice, do in individual cases—one would logically expect its defenders to choose against it sometimes. But this, to repeat, does not happen—and *that* it doesn't tells us something about how deep the roots of pro-choice sentiment really are. Abortion is not a mere "choice," in the value-free consumerist way that rhetoric frames it. No: abortion within this new faith has the status of religious ritual. It is sacrosanct. It is a communal rite—one through which, it seems safe to speculate, many people enter the secularist-progressive community of believers in the first place.

It is only if we understand the quasi-religious impulse behind the tenacity with which each and every abortion is defended that the otherwise puzzling, resolutely uncompromising character of the "pro-choice" position makes sense.

People of different views need to understand the inner logic of to-day's animus against religious believers. If the fury directed at them and their precepts could be pressed into a single word, that word would not be *theodicy*. It would not be *supersessionism*. It would not be *Pelagianism*, *Arianism*, or any of the other religious casus belli of the past. In the contemporary Western world, that single word would be *sex*. Christianity present, like Christianity past and Christianity to come, contends with many foes and countervailing forces. But its single most powerful enemy now is not the stuff of the philosophy common room. It is the sexual revolution—and the current absolutist defense of that revolution by adherents and beneficiaries.

After all, Christians and other dissidents aren't threatened with job loss because of writing in self-published books about the biblical teaching against stealing, say. Military chaplains are not being removed from office and sidelined for quoting from the book of Ruth. No, every act committed in the name of this new intolerance has a single, common denominator, which is the protection of the perceived prerogatives of the sexual revolution at all costs. The new intolerance is a wholly owned subsidiary of that revolution. No revolution, no new intolerance.

What believers and everyone else need to grasp is that contrary to what is sometimes argued among Christians themselves, secularist progressivism is not a nihilistic worldview. To the contrary: it embraces an alternative orthodoxy and a well-developed (and still developing) body of beliefs. The fundamental impulse leading to the penalizing of Christian believers today is not libertarian. It is instead neo-puritanical—that is, it is aimed at safeguarding its own body of revealed and developed truths, and at marginalizing, silencing, and punishing its traditional competitors.

This substitute religion mimics Christianity itself in many ways. It offers a hagiography of secular saints, for example, all of them patrons of the revolution: proselytizers for abortion and contraception, like Margaret Sanger and Helen Gurley Brown and Gloria Steinem; crypto-scholastics whose work is revered by generation after generation of the faithful and off-limits for intellectual revisionism, such as Alfred Kinsey and Margaret Mead; quasi-monastic ascetics, like the grim public priestesses of the National Abortion Rights Action League and Planned Parenthood and Emily's List, fighting to end the pregnancies of other women; and even foreign "missionaries," in the form of representatives within progressive charities and international bureaucracies—those who carry word of the revolution, and the sacraments of contraception and abortion, to women in poorer countries around the world.

Similarly well developed is secularist quasi-demonology, which now includes the Roman Catholic hierarchy, the spokesmen for evangelical Protestantism, legal groups involved in religious liberty cases, most political conservatives, all social conservatives, and the occasional apostate who deviates from the secularist code or, worse yet, switches sides on any article of faith concerning the revolution.

The followers of this newfound code further accept as the equivalent of Holy Writ a canon of texts and doctrine—a body of literature and commentary that cannot be questioned without risk of excommunication from the group, as we shall see later on. It is also ruled by a certain kind of logic—not Aristotelian logic, but some other kind, whose syllogisms include "*if* you are against abortion, *therefore* you are anti-woman"; "*if* you believe in Christian teaching, *therefore* you hate people who endorse same-sex marriage"; and other formulations that Aristotle himself would rule fallacious.

Whether the close overlay between the architectonic of secularist progressivism and Judeo-Christianity itself speaks to the inescapabilty of two thousand years of religious history, or rather to the resonance of those religious traditions themselves with the deepest and most ineradicable human longings for transcendence—or both—is a fascinating subject that deserves to be explored. But it seems beyond dispute that progressive ideology shares recognizable features with Judeo-Christianity, even as it repudiates all traditionalist tenets that threaten its substitute theology. The bedrock of contemporary progressivism can only be described as quasi-religious. In sum, secularist progressivism today is less a political movement than a church.

Foundational to today's secularism/progressivism is the doctrine that the Pill and its backup plan, abortion on demand, have liberated humanity—first, by freeing women from the chains of their fertility; and second, by having broken down the door to the fortress of traditional morality, after which one sexual minority after another has also been liberated. This, in a nutshell, is the new secularist faith, and in various influential quadrants, it is the culturally dominant narrative of our time. The followers of this faith are, furthermore, Kantians regarding these beliefs, in the sense that the philosopher's categorical imperative applies: that is, they believe both that they are right, and that people who disagree are wrong—and that those other people ought to think differently.

The so-called culture war, in other words, has not been conducted by people of religious faith on one side, and people of no faith on the other. It is instead a contest of *competing* faiths: one in the Good Book, and the other in the more newly written figurative book of secularist orthodoxy about the sexual revolution.

All of this exegesis is necessary to depict the combat zone where baffled religious believers now face their ascendant adversaries. Contrary to secular liberalism a generation ago, which tended to view religious belief as an anthropological artifact, progressivism today does not regard the traditional Judeo-Christian moral code as simply passé. Thanks to evolving doctrine about the sexual revolution, that code is seen instead as the equivalent of evil.

As long as there are orthodox religious believers, secularist orthodoxy is under tacit threat—just as the Puritans of three hundred years ago felt themselves menaced by the existence of Baptists, Catholics and other neighbors whose fundamental beliefs differed from their own. This is what makes the history of witch crazes and related outbreaks asserting orthodoxy against perceived threats illuminating of certain events today.

As mentioned already, community-wide moral purging of accused malefactors in the name of public safety is a phenomenon to which human beings are congenitally prone. The fabled trials of Salem in 1692, for example, were in fact a mere echo of much wider, related phenomena across the Atlantic during the centuries preceding. Legal and social convulsions over witches in Europe lasted a full four hundred years, between 1400 and 1800. Eruptions were found all over, including, among many other sites, England, France, Scandinavia, Hungary, Switzerland, Italy, and—most involved of all—Germany.

Among the suggestive facts about this history, and one bearing directly on our world in the first quarter of the third millennium, is that the witch craze was not a medieval phenomenon. It extended instead through the Renaissance, and into and beyond the Enlightenment. The authorities conducting the interrogations and trials were no shrouded illiterate peasants of the Dark Ages, but among the most educated and cultivated men of their day—including in Massachusetts, where witch hunter Cotton Mather has otherwise gone down in history as perhaps the greatest all-around genius and innovator in the New World of his time.

Similarly, the witch hunters' efforts were not exactly barbaric, but in fact relied on the most sophisticated cultural tools of the age:

English law. Far from being a provincial aberration, the phenomenon quickly entered the mainstream of the wider civilized world. As Kenneth Silverman describes in his Pulitzer Prize–winning biography, for example, Cotton Mather's 1692 book defending the trials, *Wonders of the Invisible World,* "was advertised in large type in the *London Gazette,* reviewed and summarized at length in the *London Compleat Library,* and published quickly in three English editions"—roughly the equivalent today of occupying the covers of *Time* and *Vanity Fair,* say, as well as the attention of mainstream book publishing, all at once.[12] As Mather's son, Samuel, noted in his eulogy for his father, the arch-Puritan "was had in great esteem thro' many nations in EUROPE."[13]

Transgressors of secularist orthodoxy today, like transgressors of other orthodoxies in times past, are accused of harming others in ways that are not obvious to everyone else.

The hounding of Mozilla CEO Brendan Eich, who lost his position when it was revealed that he had supported Proposition 8 in 2008 in California (as had 52 percent of the state's other voters), remains the most emblematic and cautionary example of today's secular inquisition. So egregious were the tactics forcing Eich from office that in 2014, some leaders of the movement for same-sex marriage questioned the injustice of it and published an open letter urging tolerance and civility on the inquisitors called "Freedom to Marry, Freedom to Dissent: Why We Must Have Both."[14] "Sustaining a liberal society," they noted, "demands a culture that welcomes robust debate, vigorous political advocacy, and a decent respect for differing opinions. . . . We should criticize opposing views, not punish or suppress them." The letter also noted "a worrisome turn toward intolerance" and, interestingly, "puritanism."

Though obviously a step in the right direction, and a stand for reason in the face of unreason, this letter made no lasting impact—any more than the resignation of Colonel Nathaniel Saltonstall, the single judge in Salem to oppose the unfolding trials, did anything to help the accused of his own day.[15] The lesson in both cases might be that when a moral panic is under way, it takes more than one symbolic gesture to restore civility.

Another fact redolent of the past is that the antipathy arrayed against the faithful today spills across borders. It's civilizational. In Canada, for example, a young woman who applied for a job as a river rafter with a Norwegian wilderness company was turned down following a vitriolic series of emails from the hiring manager, who disparaged her for having attended a Christian college.[16] In Canada, too, a court in 2015 upheld a decision to deny Trinity Western University, in British Columbia, accreditation for a new law school—because its campus covenant is Christian, that is, it forbids sex outside marriage.[17]

In England—which is now a virtual assembly line of such cases—a gardener who volunteered in a prison chapel was disciplined for quoting from the New Testament.[18] Several street preachers in the sceptred isle have lately been jailed for reading passages from the Bible aloud in public.[19] In one such case, a judge lectured the preacher on which exact passages in Leviticus could be read without penalty (the judge explained that Leviticus 20:13 was out of bounds, because it uses the word *abomination*). A representative from the preacher's defense team, Christian Legal Centre, responded, "The judge is effectively censoring the Bible and saying that certain verses aren't fit for public consumption."[20] In another case, a teacher in Somerset asked a sick student if she would like a prayer. The student declined, and the teacher did not pray—upon which the student's parents complained and the school fired her, with the authorities defining a prayer offer as "bullying."

Step back for a moment to consult reality. In what possible,

imaginable way does it harm anyone if someone else is praying for
them? If you are secularist, and believe that prayer itself shares the
empirical status of magic wands and unicorns, what possible grief
could come of it? At least since Diagoras of Melos in the fifth century BC, unbelievers have charged religious devotees with irratio-
nality, for believing in things unseen. But is it not commensurately
irrational to believe you are being injured by someone talking to
something that *you* don't believe exists in the first place? Who is
harmed?

Toward the end of his life, as he suffered from cancer, atheist Christopher Hitchens wrote a bemused essay reflecting on the
seeming paradox that believers around the world were writing to
say that they were praying for him.[21] Compare that relatively open
and benign gesture with the outrage that erupted online among
secularists around the country at the end of 2015, over the sug-
gestion that religious people were praying for the victims of mass
murder in San Bernardino, California. As a piece in the *Atlantic* put
it, describing this whole new line of attack on Christians known as
"prayer-shaming," "Many [progressives] turned their anger about
the shooting not at the perpetrator or perpetrators, whose identities
[were] still unknown, but at those who offered their prayers."[22] How
rational is that?

Or consider the wider, equally irrational cultural backdrop to
stories like these. Alastair Bruce, who was charged with ensuring
the historical verisimilitude of the popular show *Downton Abbey*,
explained to the *Telegraph* just how tricky it can be to portray an
early-twentieth-century English family without revealing any of the
religious practice that would have been part of daily life.[23] Meals
on the set, he explained, were always shown already under way—to
get around the perceived problem that characters would have said
grace. The word *abbey* in the show's title came in for scrutiny, over

fear that it could conjure a religious subtext. The dining room table was not even allowed to show napkins folded in the pattern traditional to the time—because it suggests a bishop's miter, apparently another possible triggering affront.

Bruce also used an interesting word to describe the force behind this historical bowdlerizing: he called it a "panic." And so it is.

What is going on out there—whether in England or Canada or the United States or elsewhere—such that even evidence of religious belief in what secularists hold to be a made-up story, summons scrutiny like this? Plainly, it's that believers are seen as a threat. But a threat to what?

The answer can only be that their religion is perceived as menacing laissez-faire sexual morality. The sexual revolution, as we have already seen, is the centerpiece of a new orthodoxy and new morality that elevates pleasure and self-will to first principles. This has become, in effect, a rival religion. That is what explains the outsize hostility toward believers who have been minding their own business, or trying to educate their children, or expressing their faith in public forums—or otherwise behaving in ways that once invited no penalties, and now do. Ubiquitously.

Because we are talking about competing religions replete with the passionate conviction that attends first principles, what's going on out there can look a lot like Salem—including the fact that it can take very little to find oneself accused and cast out these days.

In 2014, for example, a community college in Baltimore denied a prospective student admission to its radiation therapy program because when asked by interviewers, "What is the most important thing to you?" he replied "My God." In explaining the decision to deny him, the director zeroed in on those words, noting that [if you interview in the future, you may want to leave your thoughts and beliefs out of the interview process."[24]

Critics might want to rejoin that isolated anecdotes are un-revealing of a pattern. Their objection fails what we'll dub the crucifix test. If believers of other faiths were being treated this way—if "Buddha" had been the answer in Baltimore, rather than "God"—secularist progressives would be rallying from Instagram to TED talks in the name of religious liberty. Instead, we live in a world where celebrated novelist Hilary Mantel can fulminate in public to nary a peep that "[t]he Catholic Church is not an institution for respectable people"—as if she or anyone else would dare to fill in that blank with anything else.[25] It is precisely this double standard that affirms the paradigm: what's afoot is something untethered from rationalism, and more akin to what psychologists and economists know as "herd behavior," that is, the phenomenon of large numbers of people acting in the same way at the same time.[26]

Even in small things, believers are scrutinized as others are not. "I am whatever I say I am," for example, which is otherwise a governing mantra of the times, does not apply to Catholic priests. As of this writing, there are 58 "gender options" for American users of Facebook[27] (and somewhat puzzlingly, 70 such options in the United Kingdom).[28] Yet priests cannot use the title "Fr." on their personal pages, and are shut down if they attempt to—even though Facebook's official policy is that people should use the names they are known by, and even though most Catholic priests are known as "Father."[29]

Religious believers today are charged with afflicting the society around them, just in virtue of *being* who they are and thereby, it is posited, causing harm. In this sense, too, the overlay with a witch-craze dynamic fits well. As historian Hugh Trevor-Roper put it in *The European Witch-Craze of the Sixteenth and Seventeenth Centuries*, describing how the European hunts and trials originated, "the systematic mythology" was generated "by unassimilable social groups who, like the Jews and Moors of Spain, might be persecuted into outward orthodoxy, but not into social conformity, and who thereby became, as the others did not, objects of social fear."[30]

"Outward orthodoxy" without "social conformity": these are exactly the traits of today's Christians in a time of progressive ascendancy. Their antagonists might make them fall into line, or into silence, but they cannot control the Christians' dissident, hence potentially subversive, thoughts.

It's sometimes said—mainly by their opponents—that Christians should not engage in "victimology." This is but one more, albeit appreciably higher-end, attempt to silence dissent. Secular progressivism so dominates Western culture that secular academia, Hollywood, public schools, and other crucial cultural precincts aren't even contested terrain anymore. In 2012, according to the *College Fix*, 99 percent of the faculty and staff at Princeton University who donated to presidential candidates gave to Barack Obama. In 2016, 91 percent of Harvard's faculty donations went to Hillary Clinton.[31] In what possible world are circles as politically uniform as these threatened by the rare soul passing through who carries a rosary, or who stops to say grace before lunch?

Assigning powers and malignity to one's adversaries that they do not possess is evidence of collective hysteria, not enlightenment. During the Moscow show trials of 1936–38, during which every old Bolshevik except Stalin himself was swept up in a deadly farce of his devising, the accused were charged with all manner of preposterous "crimes" predicated on capacities no one had—like plotting to overthrow the Soviet Union and partition it in collusion with agents of the German and Japanese governments, something of a stretch from a Lubyanka prison cell.

Similarly, during the so-called Doctors' Plot of 1952–53, nine doctors, six of them Jews, were charged for political reasons with having committed other crimes that were quite impossible under the circumstances—of being "Vicious Spies and Killers under the Mask of Academic Physicians," as *Pravda* put it.[32] Like other episodes in the history of anti-Semitism, this one points to a universal lesson: people of little or no power can be assigned absurd capacities and influences, if that's what it takes to produce the desired punishment.

And so it is with the insistence of anti-religious enthusiasts that the faithful and their works now menace the rest of the body politic—even as the freedom of those same alleged perpetrators is being circumscribed by tools ranging from legal instruments to varieties of demonization and social disdain.

Today's accused traditionalists are also held—like the accused at Salem—to a different and lower standard of "evidence" than would be applied anywhere else.

This double standard is proof, once again, that some kind of panic rather than business as usual is under way. To quote Hugh Trevor-Roper once more on the dynamics of the European witch craze, "the mythology created its own evidence, and effective disproof became ever more difficult."[33]

The witch trials at Salem depended for their very existence on "spectral evidence," that is, evidence that did not meet ordinary standards of empiricism. This too has echoes today. People are commonly called "bigots" or "phobic," for example, simply by virtue of being religious believers. To call someone a "bigot" or "phobic" is a serious charge. It ascribes a psychology and set of motives to your opponent that denies his rationality and assigns him a malignity of motive. As Kirsten Powers has noted in her book *The Silencing*, of the equation of "Christian" and "bigot" that some activists now insist upon:

If that is true, then hundreds of millions, if not a billion, of the world's 2.2 billion Christians are bigots. It means that Bill and Hillary Clinton and Barack Obama were public bigots for most of their lives, as was virtually every Democrat holding elected office until a few years ago. As late as 2008, Barack Obama told Rick Warren that "I believe that marriage is the union between a man and a woman. Now, for me as a Christian . . . it is also a sacred union. God's in the mix."[34]

This is not to say that the faithful cannot accurately be called by other labels. For example, it would be correct to describe at least some members of today's Western religious contingent, and maybe even all of them, as "reactionaries." Many believers themselves would be the first to point out that they are *reacting* to a series of cultural transformations initiated by others, and have been for decades now. As the writer J. D. Flynn has put the point, in a response to a recent column by David Brooks in the *New York Times* suggesting that tradition-minded Christians now opt out of the political sphere:

> "Culture war" is a tendentious phrase. It presupposes—what Brooks supposes—that the religious combatants are the hawks. History suggests otherwise. Christian conservatives did not write the majority opinion in *Roe v. Wade*, which intensified hostility toward religious voices in the public square. Nor did Christian conservatives roil the country by redefining marriage or mandating the provision of contraceptives by employers.[35]

But a "reactionary" in this culture war sense does not ipso facto a "hater" or "bigot" make. The first word in quotes assumes cognizance and reason—the ability to make an argument in good faith, even if secularist opponents hold that argument to be wrong. The other words in quotes are epithets that intentionally demean and dehumanize.

Today's faithful are not pretending to have cherished beliefs as a guise under which they can at long last fulfill their ulterior dream of being "haters." They are fighting for their right to practice their most cherished beliefs as they never have had to fight before.

It is a struggle complicated by the fact that those accused of ideological wrongdoing today—like those accused of supernatural or political wrongdoing in times gone by—are at exactly the same disadvantage. Their defense depends on a cumbersome logical task: proving a negative.

"I am not a hater" is the contemporary equivalent of "I am not a witch"—or for that matter, "I am not a poisoner," "I am not plotting espionage," "I am not committing ritual murder/blood libel," or "I am not controlling the media/Pentagon/banks/world." In certain grotesque theaters of history, unfortunate human beings have been forced to issue crippling declarations like those. "I am not a hater" suffers exactly the same rhetorical burden as those other propositions. Any attempt at denial necessarily involved a compromising acceptance of the terms, making effective contradiction practically impossible—as in the well-known question "When did you stop beating your wife?"

The fact of having to deny a charge that is intrinsically odious puts the believers in a defensive and unfair position. Presumably, that is exactly why those charges of "bigot" and "hater" are made so often and insistently, whether millions of people are smeared by them or not. "You're a bigot if I say you're a bigot" is today's equivalent of "you're a witch if I say you're a witch."

It should also disquiet people outside religious circles that what's taken as "proof" of such perfidy today is not what reasonable people would regard as actual evidence. It is one thing to be videotaped flying on a broomstick, for example. It's another to have someone claim he has seen such a thing in a dream, and to have that "evidence" considered sufficient to convict. Likewise, being captured on tape or Twitter saying hateful things about sexual minorities— or anyone else—would count as empirical evidence toward being branded a "hater." But just being *accused* as such, and condemned without proof, is the stuff of kangaroo courts rather than real ones. Even so, it happens all the time now.

In Western societies today, as in Salem, "proof" of transgression—in this case, against newly built orthodoxy concerning the sexual revolution—resides not in actual evidence of wrongdoing; but rather in whether the accusations issue from a socially approved, priestly class of inquisitors. If the person throwing anti-Christian invective is "worthy"—in the sense of being believed within his *own* community of faith to have the final say on the interpretation of sexual revolution dogma—the charge of "bigot" and the rest largely sticks, evidence or no.

As fear spread in the New England community under the weight of increasing accusation, motivation to aid and otherwise supplicate the inquisitors multiplied accordingly. Some people who were initially wary of the witch trials played along anyway, aligning with the hunters in the hopes of thereby avoiding accusation themselves.

One also learns from history that as fervor for punishment spreads, it comes to engulf and consume even victims who seemed immune at the outset.

Purges that start with the marginalized and forlorn end with leaders hoist on their own pitchforks. It is the way of all revolutions; and the mini-revolution of a witch hunt or panic, against Christians or anyone else, is no exception. By the time the fury in Salem village was spent, even some formerly esteemed members of the community felt its wrath—including, most prominent of all, Minister Samuel Parris, whose parish ultimately brought charges against him for his involvement.

And so, in our own time, has anti-religious vengeance similarly sent more and more of the accused to the docket for secular heresy—including some who must never have expected to land there, beginning as they did on the "safe" side of the divide over the sexual revolution. But formerly protected status is not enough, any more than it was an effective insurance policy three centuries ago. Today's frenzy no longer limits itself to religious targets. More and more, it is also turning on its own.

Thus a first-rank feminist and founding mother of the sexual revolution itself, Germaine Greer, can be shouted down around the world for saying that surgery cannot make a man into a woman, a heresy which violates what secularist orthodoxy now holds about transgenderism—and a college can also decide to deny her an honorary degree.[36] Similarly, a prominent same-sex marriage activist in England, Peter Tatchell, can be excoriated for publishing a letter in the *Guardian* criticizing the "silencing of people" who make controversial remarks about that same phenomenon, transgenderism.[37]

More and more, some of these very leaders—those with impeccable standing yesterday—are now criticized for perceived deviations. Author and alpha blogger Andrew Sullivan, for example, whom history will record as one of the most influential advocates in the world on behalf of same-sex marriage, is now slammed by former admirers for objecting to the strong-arming of Brendan Eich, and for criticizing related attempts to squash dissent. In 2015, Sullivan made a conference appearance during which he stated that "religious freedom is fundamental to this country." This is contemporary heresy of particularly grave import, since custodians of today's new orthodoxy typically put the words "religious freedom" in sneer quotes. According to a report on Reason.com, this latest transgression resulted in "audience members on Twitter brand[ing] Sullivan's statements offensive, misogynist, and transphobic."[38]

The lesson is that under moral panic rules rather than reasonable ones, yesterday's bona fides will not count.

Or consider the case of Douglas Laycock, the University of Virginia law professor who coauthored an amicus brief in defense of same-sex marriage and otherwise established good faith among progressives—until other work of his involved religious liberty. Thereupon activists turned on him, sending him an open letter and filing a Freedom of Information Act request to see emails and phone records between the professor and groups dedicated to religious freedom. So obvious were the social mob tactics applied to Laycock's case that a writer in *Slate* could observe, "The use of FOIA—in tandem with an email campaign calling out a respected academic as a hater or an enabler of haters—is also a form of intimidation and public shaming," tactics that the piece further called "depressingly familiar."[39]

Conversely, and also suggesting that quasi-religious passion rather than reason is directing events: if the public penitence of the accused is impressive enough, at times a putative witch or wizard may be spared.

Actress Natalie Portman, for example, was sentenced to the contemporary ducking stool, that is, a social media criticism campaign, for opining in an Academy Award acceptance speech that motherhood was her "most important role" (another clear violation of sexual revolution dogma, according to which liberated women put career rather than children first).[40] Following that public relations storm, and consistent with accused sorceresses before her, the same actress performed an auto-da-fé in the public square by speaking repeatedly in public on the importance of abortion rights, including for example on behalf of President Obama's second election campaign—thereby rehabilitating herself with cultural authorities as consistent with moral protocol after all. This dynamic, of apostasy followed by public recantation, is also familiar from history.

One final reflection on today's itinerant anti-Christian irrationalism applies not to the present, but to the future. If history is any guide, as with other moral panics, the day will come when today's hounding of the Christian believers in the name of the sexual revolution will be a historical event requiring explanation upon which future generations will look in puzzlement—and worse.

Only a minority of the people accused of witchcraft in Massachusetts were actually punished for it. Schiff, for example, reports a conviction rate of 25 percent, with the majority of cases rejected for insufficient evidence. This relatively scrupulosity about evidence, ironically, stands in sharp contrast to our own time, when calumnious epithets are thrown freely, and rarely rescinded for lack of evidence. The conviction rate for heresy about the sexual revolution these days appears to be closer to 100 percent.

As an historic coda of possible interest, the aftermath of 1692 proved a somber time for the Puritans. Within just a few years of hanging the last witch, a new social consensus formed according to which the entire episode had been a massive injustice. Less than a hundred years later, John Adams would write that the trials were a "foul stain" on the country, and almost everyone else would henceforth agree. Cotton Mather, for all his other accomplishments—he was the first to introduce inoculation to the New World, among other innovations—would nonetheless go down through the centuries as one of history's villains, and his father, Increase, who eventually galvanized other ministers to cease the hunt altogether in the name of "innocent blood," is regarded in retrospect as one of the few heroes of the piece.

Whether the ongoing scare engulfing today's Christians will exact such humane revisionism in the future—that is, whether men and women now promiscuously accused of consorting with the equivalent of evil will someday have their own good names restored by penitent ex-inquisitors in the future—is an open question these days.

In the meantime, this much can be seen clearly: the era of the "culture war" dating roughly from the invention of the Pill to *Obergefell v. Hodges* has turned a new corner, around which the hunt for evildoers—defined today by self-appointed enforcers as anyone, anywhere, who questions newly revealed writ about the sexual revolution—has apparently only just begun.

3

Acclaiming "Diversity" vs. Hounding the Heretics

Begin with a pivotal cultural story that most secular readers will not have encountered before: the ongoing drive to kick Christian student groups, including and most notably the flagship club Inter-Varsity, off campuses around the country and elsewhere.

InterVarsity Christian Fellowship/USA, a Protestant evangelical organization, is one of the largest student clubs in the United States, with 985 chapters on 649 campuses.[1] Around 38 percent of its students identify themselves as "ethnic minority" or "multiracial"; particular InterVarsity subsets include Black Campus Ministries, Asian American Ministries, and Latino Fellowship. Like other Christian groups, InterVarsity also engages in charities on a broad scale, including by sending college students into urban slums around the world and by serving community residents in a long list of cities and towns around the United States.

Nonetheless, neither its minority composition nor its good works have kept InterVarsity from becoming a major target of activists who object to the group's Christianity, especially its fealty to teachings about morality. By 2014, some forty campuses had come to challenge InterVarsity's presence as a bona fide student group. In a particularly notable exercise of progressive fiat, the twenty-three colleges of California State in 2014 kicked the organization off campuses altogether.[2] In the words of the director of public affairs in the chancellor's office at California State, "InterVarsity requires leaders to sign a statement of faith, and that violates not only California state policy, but also state law. . . . They want their leaders to have specific values. If you force someone to sign a form, you are discriminating by making them say they are a Christian."

In other words, the trouble with the Christian group InterVarsity was that it wanted Christians leaders for its Christian students.

Here as elsewhere, an ideological double standard suggests itself. Are student Democratic groups forced to acquire Republicans as leaders? Is the Knitting Society ordered to include people who are allergic to yarn? Is the force of law brought to bear on the Vegan Club, to open its student leadership to carnivores? The questions are risible. But the consequences of singling out Christian student groups for state-sanctioned opprobrium are not. Such targeting ostracizes and penalizes strictly on account of religious beliefs, thereby making it harder for Christians to be Christians at college. Why the bill of attainder against them?

In 2015, the California State University system reinstated InterVarsity on nineteen campuses, clarifying that the executive order in question meant that anyone could *apply* for leadership in the group. Though a temporary victory for freedom of association, this outcome hardly dampened secularist-progressive zeal. InterVarsity continues to be challenged at other schools in California, as well as in New York, Massachusetts, Tennessee, Maine, Iowa, and Florida, in addition to the other schools that have already purged the group from the quad.

Secularist progressivism claims to champion diversity—but its activists today do not tolerate genuine diversity, including and especially in the realm of ideas, as revealed by today's legal and other attacks on Christian colleges, Christian associations and clubs, Christian schools, Christian students, and Christian homeschooling. These are bellwether ideological campaigns that have yet to garner the attention they deserve outside religious circles. Their logical conclusion is to interfere with and shut down Christian education itself—from elementary school on up to religious colleges and universities. And once more, it's legitimate to ask why such campaigns seemingly untethered from any apparent stakes are underway at all.

InterVarsity, to repeat, is only the most visible example of ongoing efforts to dismantle Christian student groups on secular campuses. The Christian group Chi Alpha, for example, has also been de-recognized at California State, Stanislaus despite more than forty years on campus, allegedly for "religious discrimination"—which is to say, for refusing to open its leadership positions to non-Christians.[3] Inter alia, students of any faith, or no faith at all, are welcome to join the group (and the other groups mentioned in this section, too). But this openness does not appease the group's ideological adversaries, who object to the fact that the group defines a practicing Christian as one who abstains from certain behaviors. As seen before, this is a stance on sexuality that neo-puritan activists find intolerable.

But who is really the intolerant party here? As one report noted, "Similar rules are regularly enforced in nonreligious student organizations, e.g., allowing fraternities to only have male leaders." The difference, it appears, is that Chi Alpha is Christian.

Another successful attempt to disrupt the free association of students who try to follow the Bible took place at Hastings College of

Law in San Francisco. There, the student chapter of the Christian Legal Society (CLS) was denied any status on the campus because—similar to the InterVarsity and Chi Alpha cases—it required that members profess their Christian convictions in writing and pledge not to engage in "unrepentant participation in or advocacy of a sexually immoral lifestyle."[4] This pledge was judged by the school to conflict with a state law requiring all registered student organizations to allow "any student to participate, become a member, or seek leadership positions, regardless of their status or beliefs."

The CLS filed suit over the denial, arguing that the university had violated its First Amendment rights. This case went all the way to the Supreme Court, which decided 5–4 in *Christian Legal Society v. Martinez* (2010) that Hastings College had not violated the First Amendment in forcing the CLS to accept members who violated its Christian moral code.[5] In other words, it found that "religious student groups have no constitutional right to discriminate against nonbelievers if they take financial support from public universities," as a *Wall Street Journal* article summarized.[6]

The divide in the *Martinez* case was notably bitter. Justice Samuel Alito's dissent, joined by Justices Roberts, Scalia, and Thomas, charged, "Today's decision rests on a very different principle: no freedom for expression that offends prevailing standards of political correctness in our country's institutions of higher learning." Adding that the majority decision "arms public educational institutions with a handy weapon for suppressing the speech of unpopular groups," Alito concluded in uncustomary dire language:

> I do not think it is an exaggeration to say that today's decision is a serious setback for freedom of expression in this country. . . . Even those who find CLS's views objectionable should be

concerned about the way the group has been treated—by Hastings, the Court of Appeals, and now this Court. I can only hope that this decision will turn out to be an aberration.[7]

Organizations and activists focused on First Amendment issues were similarly alarmed by the majority's reasoning. The Foundation for Individual Rights in Education (FIRE), which had also filed a friend of the court brief, said that it was

> deeply disappointed in the Supreme Court's ruling and view it as a dangerous threat to students' First Amendment rights. *Martinez* contradicts longstanding Supreme Court precedent upholding the freedom of association as fundamental to the exercise of one's First Amendment rights and allowing private organizations to make belief-based choices regarding membership and leadership.[8]

An article in the *Chronicle of Philanthropy* noted acerbically:

> Among the pearls of wisdom attributed to the great sage Groucho Marx was his view that "I wouldn't want to belong to any club that would accept me as a member." This week the Supreme Court solved Groucho's problem by ruling, in *Hastings Christian Fellowship v. Martinez*, that a university can force any club to let Groucho join, even if he totally disagrees with its purposes. And as a member, he can launch a hostile takeover.[9]

It is true, of course, that free-speech cases such as this one—or for that matter, other cases mentioned in this book—necessarily make their way through courts. Yet it does not take a lawyer to understand that the contraception mandate makes religious freedom take a backseat to politics, as we saw earlier on; neither is a doctorate of jurisprudence required to grasp that *CLS v. Martinez* is a disturbing harbinger of things to come. Traditionalist clubs are now singled out and undercut as others are not, all for seeking to build communities of people who share their religious views.

As James Tonkowich, former president of the Institute on Religion and Democracy, author of the recent book *The Liberty Threat*, and one more critic of the *Martinez* decision, puts the point,

> Hastings has about sixty student groups. It has denied registration based on the "all-comers" rule to exactly one. . . . Events at Hastings School of Law, Vanderbilt, and other schools are a clear illustration of how religious liberty is the first liberty. Deny religious liberty and all the other liberties collapse into rubbish. Having been denied religious liberty, CLS at Hastings and at Vanderbilt have no rights to free speech and free association.[10]

Similar efforts aimed at disrupting the student associations of certain kinds of Christians—that is, nonprogressives—also appear abroad. In 2006, the University of Edinburgh banned from its grounds a course promoting chastity taught by the club Christian Union, saying that it contradicted university values of diversity and equality. The 150-member Christian Union in Birmingham, England, has been suspended for refusing to rewrite its constitution so that non-Christians could address meetings.[11] The Christian Union at the University of Exeter has had its student guild privileges suspended for its practice of asking members to sign a declaration of faith in Jesus Christ.[12]

Again, it doesn't take a microscope to spy the animus in these cases. Rather obviously, many people today object to various constricting features of the Christian moral code, as we have seen already and will explore some more in chapter 6. But to step back from the esoterica of court documents and university minutes is to wonder, and inescapably at that: what, exactly, is wrong with Christians (or anyone else) *believing* that something is wrong? If these groups were anything but Christian in their orientation, would the bitter passion that drives case after case up the legal ladder be the same? No one forces nonbelievers to join Christian clubs. Is it fair to force the clubs to integrate nonbelievers into their leadership?

Only if the free association of Christians is threatening something very serious—like someone else's faith.

In defending the supposed rationality of the "all-comers" rule at Hastings, Chancellor Leo Martinez said in an interview with PBS that the same rule applied to everyone; that it could be used to force B'nai Brith to accept Muslim students, and a black group to admit white supremacists—even, he said, to admit members of the Ku Klux Klan.[13] Martinez was trying to prove the consistency of the rule. Leave aside for a moment the social value of that rule itself, or the spectacle of the Student Socialist Club, say, embracing members of the Republican Club forced upon them. As Tonkowich notes, even if such *were* the stated object of the rule, it isn't what happened. Only one student club at Hastings was denied registration on account of the "all-comers" policy: the traditionalist Christian one.

In the continuing inquisition of Christian student groups on campus—and *only* those groups on campus—we see once more the double standard according to which people of the Book are to be marginalized and punished by means that would cause outcry, were any other association of like-minded associates targeted thus. And once again, it's fair to ask why.

There is also the related matter of the ways in which such accepted, and acceptable, prejudice plays out against individual students.

Recall the story earlier on about the aspiring college student turned down for a radiology program who mentioned his religious faith and was criticized for doing so. As noted, it is implausible that the same outcome would have followed a reference to "God" by some other religious name. A recent book published by Harvard University Press called *Inside Graduate Admissions: Merit, Diversity, and Faculty Gatekeeping*, now raises the question of just how often a religious test—meaning an anti-Christian test—is applied behind closed doors in higher education.[14]

In that book, author Julie R. Posselt, an assistant professor at the University of Michigan, examines the inside admissions process to several PhD programs at various elite universities. Given the confidential nature of her access to such hallowed proceedings, anonymity of both the schools in question and of the faculty was guaranteed. As she notes, one episode involving a Christian applicant was especially concerning, given the questions it raised in her own mind about bias and fairness.

As an early review on *Inside Higher Ed* summarizes this episode:

> The applicant, to a linguistics Ph.D. program, was a student at a small religious college unknown to some committee members but whose values were questioned by others.
>
> "Right-wing religious fundamentalists," one committee member said of the college, while another said, to much laughter, that the college was "supported by the Koch brothers."
>
> The committee then spent more time discussing details of the applicant's GRE scores and background—high GRE scores, homeschooled—than it did with some other candidates. The chair of the committee said, "I would like to beat that college out of her," and, to laughter from committee members asked, "You don't think she's a nutcase?"

Other committee members defended her, but didn't challenge the assumptions made by skeptics.[15]

This tale, like that of the radiology hopeful, fails the aforementioned crucifix test. It is unthinkable that this same faculty team would wonder aloud whether a Sikh was a "nutcase," or whether George Soros, say, was funding higher education somewhere—let alone that a professor anywhere would dare say of a madrassa or yeshiva that "I'd like to beat that college out of her."

In response to Posselt's anecdote, David French, a lawyer, former law professor, and former president of FIRE, has relayed another, similar story about anti-Christian bias. He notes: "This was remarkably similar to my own experience fifteen years ago, when I intervened to stop a similar incident while serving on the admissions committee while teaching at Cornell Law School":

> In one of the most memorable incidents [of ideological cleansing], the committee almost rejected an extraordinarily qualified applicant because of his obvious Christian faith (he'd attended a Christian college, a conservative seminary, and worked for religious conservative causes). In writing, committee members questioned whether they wanted his "Bible-thumping" or "God-squadding" on campus.[16]

The sense that people of the Book may not be exactly clubbable, or "our sort," appears to lurk in other kinds of academic gatekeeping, too. In 2016, for example, a book dealing in part with fetal development made the rounds of a faculty committee meeting at a prestigious academic press. The subject of abortion was mentioned. In response, one professor joked, "Do they [that is, pro-lifers] even read?"[17]

Anecdotes like these are windows not only into biased psyches of some parochial academics. They also illuminate indirectly other scenes now playing out across kitchen tables around the country: the conversations being had among Christian families as they face the reality of soft discrimination, and feel forced to weigh their religious faith against the question of their children's greater good.

This is another, insidious way in which religious freedom is being curtailed these days: by social stigma. If families have to think twice about educating their children in religious institutions for fear that the choice will cripple those children's prospects later in the secular world, how is that *not* a gross compromise of religious liberty? As author Rod Dreher summarized the dilemma in a piece titled "Grad School: No Christians Need Apply":

> What happens when your kid can't get into graduate school because she has attended a Christian college identified by educational elites as a bigot factory? It's not persecution, of course, but these are the kinds of choices that orthodox Christians are going to face very soon. Will they, and their kids, be strong enough to give up dreams of reaching the top, because it's not worth compromising their faith? [18]

Related intolerance is also displayed in other efforts aimed at preventing the transmission of Christian thought. Consider the purposiveness with which some progressive standard-bearers now attack, of all things, homeschooling—that is, the practice now adopted by millions of American families for educating children outside of government institutions.

Such ideological resentment of the idea of parents teaching their own children may come as a surprise to many readers. As such, it is one more initiative committed in progressivism's name about which

other Americans on that side of the aisle may themselves be unaware.

Let's stop again and reflect for just a moment. Surely most open-
minded men and women, if pressed for an opinion, would agree
that the way other people choose to educate their own children is
not exactly everyone else's business. Wouldn't we? Some might also
think to admire the parents who have the stamina and conviction
to shoulder that heavy responsibility. After all, and as officials with
experience of recruiting in higher education know well—alongside
nonofficials watching national spelling bees and geography bees
and other competitions—homeschooling often produces outstanding students. That's why special efforts are made, including on elite
campuses, to entice those cream-of-the-crop students who learned
at home.[19]

Here as elsewhere in our examination of anti-Christian soldiers,
the first salient fact is that activists even *have* a lockstep position
against homeschooling, rather than a diversity of views. Here as
elsewhere, *diversity* is a thin word—whereas the thick reality of intolerance is something very different.

For while "homeschooling" is the ostensible target, the real reason parental freedom to educate one's own children irks today's activists is that the majority of homeschooled children are in Christian
families. Homeschooling is one more lightning rod for the peculiarly
intense hostility radiating from supposedly progressive quadrants.

Consider a recent article at *Slate*, forthrightly titled "Liberals,
Don't Homeschool Your Kids: Why Teaching Children at Home
Violates Progressive Values."[20] Or this tendentious phrasing from
another recent article at *Salon*:

> Religion as child abuse has, of course, always formed the
> mainstay of faith. A desire to indoctrinate the unsuspecting

young in faith's dark, lurid dogmas before science, reason, and the enlightening joys of secularism take over and help them mature into healthy adults has for decades motivated a controversial homeschooling movement afflicting some 2.5 million children in the United States. . . . Homeschooling amounts to allowing the faith-deranged to infect their young with their disorder.[21]

If other parents around America were following a curriculum laden with some of progressivism's greatest hits—say, via a canon that included works by Arthur Miller, Richard Hofstadter, Richard Dawkins, Christopher Hitchens, and Philip Pullman—it's safe to bet that the American Civil Liberties Union and like-minded allies would be defending the right of those parents to educate their children as they see fit. But if instead you're poring over classics of Judeo-Christianity at the kitchen table, then charges of undermining public education—even society itself—will be thrown your way. Homeschooling must be assaulted, so runs the ideological reasoning, because it's something *Christians* do.

Thus Richard Dawkins, among other new atheists, has repeatedly attacked the right of parents to school their children, by likening religious education to "child abuse."[22] Nor is faith-based education outside the home acceptable, either; Dawkins has made a documentary against religious schools. Bill Maher, similarly, has attacked former Senator Rick Santorum's practice of homeschooling as "the Christian madrassa that is the family living room." A homeschooler cannot even be named to a state education board, as happened in Texas in 2015, without objection from somewhere on the supposedly more tolerant side of the spectrum.[23]

There is scholarly literature aimed against homeschooling, too—not on the grounds that homeschooling is academically inadequate, but for the specific reason that it's done by Christians.

Consider a 2010 article by a professor of law at George Washington University, which opens on this prejudicial note: "This Essay explores the choice many traditionalist Christian parents (both fundamentalist and evangelical) make to leave public schools in order to teach their children at home, *thus in most instances escaping meaningful oversight*" (emphasis added). Though surely not intended, the use of the word *oversight* is a red flag—one signaling that there's a need to keep closer track of those sneaky Christians, as though they are up to something baleful. Who would think to worry about that—apart from people who regard religious believers as some kind of rival force, something dangerous, subversive, and in need of closer scrutiny?

After acknowledging that the article's questioning of homeschooling has nothing to do with academic merit, the author goes on to observe that "my comments focus on civic education in the broadest sense, which I define primarily as exposure to the constitutional norm of tolerance. I shall argue that the growing reliance on homeschooling comes into *direct conflict with assuring that children are exposed to such constitutional values*" (emphasis added).[24]

Would anyone fret on public record about whether children were being "exposed to constitutional values" if they were being homeschooled by members of MoveOn.org, or the ACLU, or Friends of the Earth? What about education via yeshivas or madrassas—are these kinds of schooling, too, held up as possible breeding grounds for anticonstitutional subversives? Likely not. If homeschooling weren't a Christian thing, it's hard to imagine it being attacked.

In his 2011 book, *The Rage Against God*, author Peter Hitchens (brother of the late Christopher Hitchens) also notes the phenomenon of progressive agitation over education at home. He devotes a chapter to comparing the steady delegitimation of religion under communism with the ascendancy today of calls to deny parental rights to instruct their children (Hitchens spent three years in the Soviet Union as a correspondent, in the years leading up to the Cold War's end). To observe that connection is not to posit a moral equivalence between today's progressives and yesterday's communists. It is simply to note, as Hitchens does, that "[t]he use of this claim that religious instruction is a form of child abuse . . . is propaganda, not reason." [25]

Here, as in other attempts to shut down free speech and free exercise, voices raised in the name of progressivism are channeling fundamentally illiberal agendas.

Thinkers across the pond have gone even further in their rationalizations for depriving Christian parents of educational options than have their American counterparts. Psychologist Nicholas Humphrey, for example, who is praised by Dawkins, offered the following blueprint in a public speech:

> Children, I'll argue, have a human right not to have their minds crippled by exposure to other people's bad ideas—no matter who these other people are. Parents, correspondingly, have no god-given licence to enculturate their children in whatever ways they personally choose: no right to limit the horizons of their children's knowledge, to bring them up in an atmosphere of dogma and superstition, or to insist they follow the straight and narrow paths of their own faith. In short, children have a right not to have their minds addled by nonsense. *And we as a society have a duty to provide it.* (emphasis added) [26]

In the end, the ideological combativeness toward homeschooling is instructive for several reasons.

First, it reveals once more an ideology that cannot bear intellectual competition. Here as elsewhere, the "marketplace of ideas" metaphor honed by John Milton and John Stuart Mill, and injected into American jurisprudence by Justice Oliver Wendell Holmes—a model of neutrality and openness that liberals as well as conservatives have embraced for almost a hundred years—is repudiated by people acting in progressivism's name. In reality, their anti-Christian combustion drives toward cultural monopoly. The left/radical National Education Association, for example, passed among its 2014–15 resolutions this ukase: "Homeschooling programs based on parental choice cannot provide students with a comprehensive educational experience."[27] "Cannot"? Ever?

Note the distinguishing characteristic of that sentence: its unnecessary absolutism. Surely the NEA could acknowledge that not all homeschooling is disallowed—couldn't they? The blanket statement allowing no exceptions is another clue: what's being defended against is something fiercely held, an alternative faith.

Second, skepticism about the idea that Christians are qualified to teach in the first place reveals again a unique condescension toward people of faith—or at least, *some* people of faith, that is, the people whose faith it is permissible to attack. If the majority of homeschooling families were Shinto or Confucian or Hindu, would they excite the same negative passions? To grasp just how safe it is to single out certain Christians instead, consider these instances of local color.

Shortly after 9/11, an emergency drill for public school students in Muskegon County, Michigan, cast homeschoolers in the role of terrorists. According to the local paper:

> In the exercise, a domestic terrorist group—dubbed Wackos Against Schools and Education—plants a bomb on a public school bus loaded with students. According to materials handed

out to explain the fake scenario, the "Wackos" believe everyone should be home-schooled.[28]

A few years after "Wackos," a New Jersey public high school conducted a different mock hostage-taking drill—this time with detectives playing gunmen who were fundamentalists, motivated by their refusal to separate church and state. According to the script, one of the terrorists is motivated by the fact that his daughter had been sent home for praying before class.[29]

In both cases, what's noteworthy is the trope of practicing Christians as a threat to public safety. It is hard to imagine anyone drafting a similar scenario with atheists in the villainous lead—or pro-abortion activists, or feminists, or Native Americans, or, in fact, anyone *but* practicing Christians.

Third, the attack on homeschooling illuminates another fault line visible elsewhere: a gaping lack of empathy. Just as the poor are made to take a backseat to the sexual revolution, so does the political hammering of educational choice subvert progressivism's claim to represent a spirit of compassion.

What, after all, has given rise to that countercultural movement in the first place? In many cases, it is mediocre government schools: institutions where violence has become chronic, and whose ethical culture makes them little more than day prisons. Yet activists opposed to this grassroots response seem not to see the children who are victimized, bored, bullied, or mistaught in worse-off public schools. The last two progressive presidents, Bill Clinton and Barack Obama, both opted out of the District of Columbia's government schools by sending their own children to elite private ones. What about other parents who *also* don't want their children in public schools, but don't have the wherewithal of American presidents?

To return to a point made earlier, the explosion of homeschooling is also related to the promulgation of a secularist, anti-religious agenda in public schools for many years now—a campaign that has broadly succeeded. No less a progressive icon than former New York governor Mario Cuomo sent his own children to Catholic school because "the public schools inculcate a disbelief in God," as he said at a dinner reported by journalist Fred Barnes.[30] And that was decades ago.

Religious parents have lost on school prayer, lost on sex education, lost on the kind of secularist and left-leaning books that dominate public school curricula, and lost on being treated as equal partners in public school communities. Their Bible is so toxic that a substitute teacher can now be suspended for giving one to a curious student—not because the teacher was evangelizing, but because the student asked about a phrase he had invoked from it ("The first shall be the last, and the last shall be the first").[31] By that standard, inter alia, goodbye to Shakespeare and plenty else. One cannot read the canonical works of Western literature without a working knowledge of the Bible.

And now, having won the very culture war battles that sent Christians streaming out of public schools in the first place, their triumphant opponents want to undercut one system built as a refuge from all that: homeschooling.

Across the country, for example, the issue arises of whether homeschooled children should be allowed access to sports and other activities—for which their parents pay mandatory taxes. Yet activists fight these initiatives, too, in the hope of forcing such children back to public institutions; in the words of one more NEA proclamation: "home-schooled children should not participate in any extracurricular activities in the public schools."[32] This is punishment in action, unleashed against a cultural minority.

Here as elsewhere, the desire to cut Christianity down to size tears at the very roots of progressivism itself. One of the greatest liberal thinkers of all time, John Stuart Mill, was taught at home by his father—"homeschooled"—from the earliest age. As Mill wrote in *On Liberty*, "A general State education is a mere contrivance for moulding people to be exactly like one another; and as the mold in which it cast them is that which pleases the predominant power in the government." This architect of human freedom would find the coercion and narrow-mindedness of some of his supposed political fellows today intolerable.

On July 1, 2014, President D. Michael Lindsay of the evangelical Gordon College, writing as an individual rather than as a college official, signed a letter along with fourteen other Christians, asking for a "religious exemption" to the president's planned executive order banning sexual orientation discrimination by federal contractors.[33] Gordon is a flagship Christian college in Massachusetts regarded across the country as one of evangelical Protestantism's premier institutions. As writer David French noted in *National Review* at the time, even leftist standard-bearer Elizabeth Warren had supported a religious exemption in such cases in 2013.[34] Nonetheless, by July 2014, President Lindsay's request was manifestly judged to be beyond the pale.

Thus, Gordon's policy requiring students and employees to limit sexual activity to marriage became a target of ire, and the college was threatened on various fronts with delegitimation in ways that no secular college in the country has had to face. As French summarizes,

> In an act of pure moral grandstanding, in July—just eight days after President Lindsay signed the letter to President Obama—the

city of Salem suspended a long-term contract with Gordon that had allowed the college to use the city-owned Town Hall—a spiteful act. . . . In late August, the Lynn School Committee—a nearby school district—ended an eleven-year relationship with the school and refused to accept Gordon College students as student-teachers in its system. . . . Then, in September, Gordon's accreditor, the New England Association of Schools and Colleges, announced that it had met to consider whether "Gordon College's traditional inclusion of 'homosexual practice' as a forbidden activity" violated the association's standards for accreditation.[35]

In other words, 312 years after the witch trials, a new hunt for imagined demons was on in Salem and environs.

In 2015, following a year of intense pressure, Gordon College retained its accreditation, thanks in part to concessions made by the school (including the establishment of a "Working Group" that would bring in speakers who rejected traditional Christian teaching). Whether the stay will prove lasting or temporary is an open question; as one writer in *First Things* observed, the board's statement that it was "not making any changes at this time to the College's Life and Conduct Statement" did seem to raise the question, "why 'at this time' "?[36] Meanwhile, two points about this textbook attempt to intimidate a Christian college stand out.

First, the episode confirms that secularist orthodoxy about sex trumps efforts to help the poor. The syllogism is simple. Unless material resources are infinite, as they are not, then to discredit and impede people who help the poor is to hurt the poor—in this case, public school students who would have benefited from that tutoring.

And Gordon's students do not only tutor in public schools. That is just part of a broad service commitment for which the school is known, and is one of the features that draws Christian students there in the first place. "[I]ts students are actively involved in local and national mentoring and aid programs and its commitment to helping the poor and needy is exemplary," as the *New Boston Post* put it in a postmortem on the attack. "Gordon students spend time in the poorest regions of the world, providing orphan care and instruction, assisting in construction projects, and volunteering in leper colonies. Their commitment and dedication to charity is unassailable." [37] Undercutting their college, giving it a black eye in public opinion, also tacitly undercuts good works like these.

Second, the hammer-and-tongs approach to Gordon is a particularly instructive example of the various tools for intimidation that can be deployed against unrepentant churchgoers these days. In addition to the overt campaign against accreditation, parallel attempts were made to destroy the college's reputation in the field of public opinion—again, with no outcry from practically anyone outside Protestant evangelical circles.

The athletic director at Emmanuel College, for example—a self-described Catholic school—announced that it would no longer play in contests against the ideological untouchables.[38] The head of a local school board compared Gordon students to the Ku Klux Klan.[39] The well-known Peabody Essex Museum, in Salem, ended its relationship with the college.[40]

It is true that left-leaning Massachusetts is particularly frigid territory for an evangelical community. But Gordon is no isolated case. A similar secularist effort at undercutting another religious school—The King's College in New York City, another small, classically grounded evangelical institution of higher learning—preceded it by almost ten years.

In 2005, a liberal member of the New York State Board of Regents and former president of New York University determined to question King's credentials for accreditation on several grounds.[41]

He challenged the relatively small size of the library—as if King's were not across the street from one branch of the New York Public Library, and seven blocks from the main building. As author and social scientist Stanley Kurtz pointed out at the time in an analysis of that challenge, "That gives King's a better library than all but a handful of colleges and universities in New York State." [42]

This member of the Board also questioned whether the school's very name was confusing, on the ground that "King's College" had long ago been the name of what is now Columbia University—as if anyone, anywhere, wouldn't know the difference. In the end, the New York State Board of Education itself recommended five years of accreditation for the college, but the Board of Regents voted for only one, a move that made both recruitment of future students and fund-raising far more problematic, as the administration complained. [43]

If readers can imagine a similar hairsplitting attack by authorities on any *secular* college in America, then this is *not* a case for the history books of anti-evangelical bias. And if parallel cases don't leap to mind, fair-minded people of all political inclinations should be feeling uneasy. In the end, the campaign against King's ended in a rout for the school's detractors, but not before confirming something that members of the college's community would not previously have known, that is, just how forceful the ire against their mere existence could become.

Joining Stanley Kurtz, who called the strong-arming of King's "the worst sort of blue-state bigotry," Peter Wood, the college's provost—who had previously spent two decades at Boston College—reflected:

> In moving to King's, I expected an opportunity to engage
> in the constructive work of shaping a curriculum and building

a faculty without the constant interruptions of controversy. . . . I hadn't counted on just how much New York state was going to trouble itself over the existence of a college like King's. . . . Instead of keeping King's out on its scenic bluff overlooking the Hudson 30 miles north of New York City, [its president] moved it into the Empire State Building. That move broke what I now see as a tacit understanding. Protestant evangelical colleges belong upstate— or better yet, out of state, somewhere in the vicinity of large belt buckles and lowing livestock.[44]

Beyond the testing of King's and Gordon, still other authorities want to discredit religious higher education altogether. Writing in the *Chronicle of Higher Education* in 2014, a professor at the University of Pennsylvania called accreditation for *any* Christian college a "scandal," adding that "[p]roviding accreditation to colleges like [evangelical Protestant] Wheaton [College] makes a mockery of whatever academic and intellectual standards the process of accreditation is supposed to uphold."[45] Trinity Western University in Canada has likewise been embroiled for years in a battle to keep its accreditation—because its community members pledge not to have sex outside traditional marriage.

To ask the obvious question: exactly *whose* schools are being attacked as unworthy, substandard, and undeserving of recognition?

Christians' schools, that's whose—not progressive flagships like Bennington, or Middlebury, or Sarah Lawrence. If religious traditionalists were fanning out to campaign against schools dominated by other canons, cacophony would resound from Cupertino to Bangor. But because the prejudice propelling these attacks has Christianity in its sights, no one outside religious circles objects.

Here again, empathy from secular and progressive people who do *not* want to shut down religious education altogether, and who *do* believe that other citizens should be free to choose the kind of colleges they want, would be a vital addition to this conversation. There is an elementary question of fairness here. Christian activists are not trying to shutter secular schools—but some progressive activists are trying to put Christian schools out of business. Can't tolerant people have a problem with that, even if they aren't believers?

Activists claim that the purpose of religious exemptions is to discriminate against certain kinds of students; but that charge is inaccurate. The *intention* behind requesting religious exemptions, and an obvious one at that, is not to discriminate against anyone. The *intention* is to create communities whose members unite around certain Christian beliefs, such as reserving sex for marriage, and who pledge to behave accordingly. Sexual disposition, or "orientation," is not grounds for disqualification. Sexual behavior outside of marriage, understood as Christianity has always understood marriage, is.

Plainly, activists and enforcers of small-s secularist writ do not want Christian schools to be free to create a community where their beliefs can be practiced. The question that needs to be asked is this: Does every other member of the secular-progressive alliance agree that Christian schools should be forcibly prohibited from creating communities that are Christian in nature—or not?

Efforts to impede religious education are also part of an ongoing paradox. It is not Christian colleges that have made a habit of harassing and intimidating speakers who represent different points of view; it is *non*religious campuses.

When socialist presidential candidate Bernie Sanders gave a speech in September 2015 at Liberty University, media accounts, including in the *New York Times*, took note of how courteous and polite the student body was, and how they unfailingly applauded a speaker who acknowledged at the outset disagreeing with their views profoundly.[46] The hostile reception certain other thinkers are guaranteed these days, just by setting foot on secular campuses, was not mentioned.

The circumscribing of free speech on secular quads has blossomed into a spectacle so operatic that it has lately given rise to book-length treatments. In *The Silencing*, Kirsten Powers catalogs scores of examples and emphasizes the religious double standard that dominates. "To the illiberal left," she summarizes, "Islam cannot be criticized without recourse to bigotry; on the other hand, the illiberal left seems to regard Christianity as the very definition of bigotry."[47]

Certainly it is true that devotees of the Good Book are greeted by an especially bilious class of protester. Thus, for example, University of Tulsa students protested a former self-professed lesbian turned Christian—on the grounds that calling something "sinful" is "thinly veiled hate speech," as one leader of the protest explained.[48] Similarly, when Jennifer Roback Morse—a former Ivy League professor and head of the Ruth Institute, a nonprofit dedicated to traditional Christian teaching—appeared at the University of California, Santa Barbara, twenty students interrupted her talk with chants, waving signs inscribed with various obscenities.[49] When Christian speaker Ravi Zacharias spoke at the University of Pennsylvania, a local atheist group handed out bingo-style cards mocking the speaker to every student who entered the hall.[50] The list could go on.

In 2013, Trinity College at Oxford hosted the legal group Christian Concern for a three-day conference on "How to Engage the Secular Culture." Again, vitriol ensued, with protesters charging that the group was (apparently in earnest) "intolerant." Since Christian

Concern's supporters include former archbishop of Canterbury George Carey, among other leaders inside the Anglican Communion and out, it's hard to see attacks on the group as anything *but* an expression of anti-Christian prejudice.

One can empathize with the bewildered college president responsible for the invitation, who later said he had "no idea there was anything controversial about them."[51] He did not realize, as administrators from Sydney to London and across the United States are now learning, that in many corridors of power and cachet these days, to be Christian is by definition controversial.

In short, H. L. Mencken memorably defined puritanism as "the haunting fear that someone, somewhere, may be happy." By similar logic, neo-puritanism appears to be the haunting fear that someone, somewhere may be a Christian exercising the right to free association with other Christians. To survey today's attacks is to understand that religious traditionalists have reason to believe that they are being singled out for ideological marksmanship as others are not.

That double standard offers one more opportunity for genuinely tolerant people to distance themselves from what is being committed in progressivism's name. It would be valuable to hear from people of the left who do *not* want to stigmatize Christian students, or rid the world of Christian colleges, campus clubs, schools, and homeschooling.

The trouble is that many people *do* want these things—and the silence of their fellows gives breakaway inquisitors carte blanche to do what they're doing.

Surveying the extraordinary success of the contemporary progressive agenda not only in the United States but elsewhere in the West, people of divergent perspectives have paused to wonder how so much seems to have happened so quickly. It's a fascinating question, and the analyses to come will make absorbing reading. Yet part of the answer is visible already. That's the fact that influential activists enforce orthodoxy against religious believers (and others) by tactics that should be ruled out in an open society. As more examples in the following chapter go to show, the ghost of progressivism present sometimes looks less like Martin Luther King Jr. than it does Senator Joseph McCarthy.

4

Civil Rights Talk vs. McCarthyite Muscle

In August 2012, a gunman entered the office building in downtown Washington, D.C., that houses the Family Research Council (FRC), a Christian organization dedicated to traditional moral teaching. By his own account, available on video, he was alerted by secular progressive "watchdog" groups, including the Southern Poverty Law Center, that painted the FRC as a "hate group." The shooter explained that this made him intend to kill as many of its members as he could, as he later told the FBI.[1] In the event, he fired at and hit a security guard, who disarmed him before his dream of mass murder could be fulfilled.

As was noted at the trial, where the gunman was given a twenty-five-year sentence, without that guard's quick action, in all likelihood the result would have been a bloodbath. Moreover, the would-be killer intended to move on to attack another Christian group, the Traditional Values Coalition, that had been similarly designated by progressive watchdogs for "hating." Yet social media and other denigrations of religious believers as "haters" and "bigots" and the rest by so-called watchdog groups roll on—exactly as if words mean nothing.

The 2012 shooting at the FRC and its aftermath reveal, first, that Christians may have a point in thinking that they are held in lower regard by many progressive Americans than are others. Imagine the near miss in this case had the shooting happened in one of the repositories of secularist progressivism in downtown Washington, D.C. Publicity would have unfurled nonstop; the websites listing individuals and groups as "haters" would have been called out across the country; and no doubt a national moment of "soul-searching" would have been demanded, as often follows public tragedies in this country—and rightly so, because many citizens would have been shocked by the idea that just having convictions that differ from other people's can be a dangerous thing.

In fact, readers do not have to imagine such a comparison. One is already at hand. In November 2015, a gunman in Colorado killed a police officer and injured several other people at a Planned Parenthood clinic. Secularists and progressives across the media immediately connected dots between that gunman's motivation on the one hand, and undercover sting videos of the abortion industry released by the Center for Medical Progress throughout the preceding months.

Writing in the *Guardian* after those shootings, for example, and calling attention to extremist rhetoric by some pro-lifers, one writer stated, "Words matter. When we dehumanize people—when we call them demons, monsters, and murderers—we make it easier for others to do them harm. Let's not pretend that we don't know that."[2] Another observed similarly in the *Washington Post* that, "Leaders incite and inflame with fiery speeches and threatening words. . . . They use violent language. And they unleash the worst impulses of the unstable and the unmoored."[3] Another in *Slate* also criticized pro-lifers for inflammatory rhetoric, adding that "it defies common sense to insist that there is no connection between political rhetoric and political violence—to insist, essentially, that there is no such thing as incitement."[4]

But if words do count, and if the power of the Internet, especially, means that everyone needs to be more careful about what they say, it's fair to ask for consistency. The enforcement wing of today's anti-religious alliance bristles with opposition researchers, self-appointed watchdog groups, and other activists who work to stigmatize religious believers in the public square. Examples abound.

One such watchdog group, for example—"Right Wing Watch," a "project" of People for the American Way—is "dedicated to monitoring and exposing the activities of the right-wing movement."[5] Its website posts a long list of congressmen, journalists, authors, and other individuals named and sometimes pictured as well. These miscreants are charged with "hatred," "bigotry," "viciousness," "lies," and other inflammatory accusations.

The Southern Poverty Law Center (SPLC), another band of enforcers—"dedicated to fighting hate and bigotry"—similarly posts "Extremist Files" of individuals and groups.[6] These "files" indiscriminately list, for example, independent-minded social scientist Charles Murray and Christians like those at the Family Research Council alongside neo-Nazis, Ku Klux Klan leaders, Holocaust deniers, and other people motivated by racial and other animosity. Using blood-red graphics and repeated blaring of the categories HATE & EXTREMISM and THE YEAR IN HATE, as well as features like a HATE MAP and HATE BLOG and other repetitions of the word HATE, the SPLC website seethes with animosity of its own.

The SPLC, Right Wing Watch, and other watchdog groups also single out for vituperation certain legal organizations that aid plaintiffs in religious liberty cases. Under the banner HATE WATCH, for example, SPLC reports that one such group of attorneys, Liberty Counsel, is representing one of the members of the Center for Medical Progress indicted in Texas in connection with the undercover Planned Parenthood abortion sting videos. Obviously, to announce such news under HATE WATCH is to imply that there is no valid or principled reason for representing such a client. The insinuation is that legal representation can only be ascribed to a nefarious impulse.

In a publication called " 'Religious Liberty' and the Anti-LGBT Right," for example (the quotes around "Religious Liberty" are theirs), the SPLC attacks the Alliance Defending Freedom (ADF), Liberty Counsel, and the Becket Fund for Religious Liberty—organizations of lawyers that have represented clients in religious-liberty cases.[7] It accuses these groups of contributing to an "atmosphere of bigotry and discrimination" and of being "extremists" who purvey "excuses to discriminate against other Americans for who they are." It also slaps epithets on these attorneys reminiscent of the patois of anti-Semitism, including "clever" and "cynical."

To be accused of reflexively and irrationally hating *anyone*, let alone a purported whole class of people, is a grave charge. It is both personally injurious and could also have professional and other momentous repercussions. So let's step back and think about that for a moment.

The representation of clients like the pastors in Houston mentioned earlier, or the florist in Washington State who declined on grounds of religious belief to make an arrangement for a same-sex wedding, or similar plaintiffs, is *legal representation*. This is the right of every American.

Moreover, liberalism has prided itself historically on its tradition of defending the outcast and despised. Think of Atticus Finch facing down a racist justice system in *To Kill a Mockingbird*, or radical lawyer William Kunstler defending members of the Black Panthers and Weather Underground. Defending the right of persons (especially those who belong to a disenfranchised minority) to hold and express unpopular opinions used to be the first tenet of the liberal catechism. If legal representation of people whose opinions are unpopular now makes organizations of lawyers into de facto "hate groups," then something about a supposedly open society has gone terribly wrong.

Rather obviously, there is an important clash of goods and principles involved in these and other cases concerning religious liberty. Those need to be adjudicated in courts, and in the court of public opinion, with due respect for the rights and liberties at stake on both sides. Attempts to delegitimize legal representation for one side of this dispute is both wrong, and damaging to society.

If liberal attorneys who defended, say, inmates at Guantanamo Bay were being reviled as bigots and extremists, "clever" and "cynical," that would be wrong. If organizations that typically represent the handicapped, or unions, or pro-abortion groups were being targeted and called inflammatory names, that too would be wrong. Consistency demands that when the legal groups representing clients in religious liberty cases are attacked in these ways, this is wrong as well.

The Human Rights Campaign (HRC), another nonprofit watchdog group on the left, also demonizes the Alliance Defending Freedom as "extremist," "dangerous," and "hateful."[8] To repeat: attempts to discredit lawyers siding with plaintiffs whose views other people disagree with have no parallel anywhere else on the political spectrum. Child molesters, mafiosi and serial killers are allowed representation not only without retribution, but on the shared understanding that it's constitutionally destructive to undermine the rule of law by trying to discredit or intimidate legal representatives. In 2000, for example, when the ACLU defended the North American Man-Boy Love Association (NAMBLA), which advocates sex between adults and children, Harvey Silvergate, an ACLU Board member, explained that decision by noting, "The Constitution is for everybody. But there are some people who just don't understand that and never will."[9]

Yet treating Christian lawyers or lawyers aligned with Christians as if they were subversives has become routine.[10]

The National Abortion Rights Action League (NARAL) also singles out individuals who disagree with that organization's platform. Consider the experiences of Teresa Stanton Collett, professor of law at the (Catholic) University of St. Thomas in Minnesota, and a consultant to the Pontifical Council on the Family in Rome. She has made various arguments to which NARAL objects, including defending statutes that set surgical standards for abortion clinics and require abortion doctors to have admitting privileges at the local hospital (which one might think that advocates of safe and legal abortion would approve).[11] Collett has also appeared at pro-life events, and defended a state law requiring pre-abortion ultrasounds in Oklahoma.

In response, NARAL has made and circulated an attack video calling the law professor a "fake expert."[12] It also disseminated an online petition aimed at discrediting the professor with her employer ("tell University of St. Thomas to take action and stop letting Teresa Collett use their name while providing any type of testimony!").[13] Nor was bullying limited to the Internet. Canvassers went door-to-door in the St. Thomas University neighborhood with the same petition—at one point trying to collect a signature from a priest at a local rectory.[14]

For another glimpse of how attempts at intimidation play out on the receiving end, consider some of the experiences of Ryan T. Anderson, an author and senior research fellow at the Heritage Foundation whose work focusing on religious liberty and marriage has been cited by Justice Samuel Alito and Justice Clarence Thomas in Supreme Court decisions.[15]

A scholar with a PhD in political economy from Notre Dame who drew attention early on as a Phi Beta Kappa graduate of Princeton and research assistant to Princeton's renowned Professor Robert P. George, Anderson may seem an unlikely target for systematic venom. But neither his civility nor his bookishness have spared him the rancor hurled at some Christian thinkers these days. His public appearances are now lightning rods for ideological malevolence of a kind without counterpart elsewhere on the spectrum.

In 2013, for example, during an appearance on *Piers Morgan Live* in which he defended the same view of marriage that Hillary Clinton and Barack Obama held until right before the case of *United States v. Windsor* (2013), Anderson was made to sit in the audience surrounded by hostile viewers as Morgan and arch-progressive television personality Suze Orman sat on stage, and literally talked down to him. In 2015, another appearance to discuss Indiana's Religious Freedom Restoration Act (RFRA) on Ed Schultz's *The Ed Show* on MSNBC took a noteworthy turn when Schultz, on air, called Indiana governor Mike Pence a "homophobe." When Anderson objected that this was a slur hurled with no evidence to back it up, Schultz responded angrily, "Cut his mike. Cut his mike off." And the show did.[16]

In a prolonged Twitter exchange in 2015 with a *New York Times* reporter, during which Anderson repeatedly made the case for civility and respect for opposing perspectives, the reporter responded with "Why shouldn't I call you names?" and "Civility is not always a virtue" and "Some people are deserving of incivility" and "obviously some policy views render people unworthy of respect." Anderson explained, "people are always worthy of respect, even if their policy views are misguided. Nothing renders people 'unworthy of respect.'" He continued: "I think even when we vehemently disagree with someone the person still has innate human dignity, still worthy of respect."[17]

Other social punishments have also been meted out. Before oral arguments at the Supreme Court in the case of *Obergefell*, the *Washington Post* ran a front-page profile of Anderson.[18] When his high school alma mater in Baltimore posted a link for the *Post* story on their Facebook page, it was immediately taken down because of complaints from students and alumni who said that the school wouldn't link to a racist alumnus; why then should it link to Anderson? The school took the article down so as not to "hurt" anyone.[19] Overlooked, of course, was how this might "hurt" students attending the school who actually agreed with Anderson. But the wider point about retail intimidation like this is damning: if you value your position in society, you'd better not be an unapologetic Christian.

When a traditionalist group in Bermuda, Preserve Marriage, tried to host Anderson for a speech, the Hamilton Princess hotel canceled the event saying it wouldn't host "anti-diversity" events, and the talk had to be moved elsewhere.[20] A spokesman for Preserve Marriage immediately pointed out that the Princess was "operating under the false idea that banning a presentation results in upholding diversity, when in reality it violates the definition and practice of diversity in every form." But as case after case goes to show, "diversity" for progressive activists intent on railroading traditionalists and non-progressive scholars does not include voices with which they disagree.

In the United States and other open societies, citizens are

supposed to welcome full-throated debate in legal and political matters, and to let the most persuasive side win. What does not comport with traditional ideas of fair play is an attempt to win the debate by stigmatizing one side as "haters," questioning the legitimacy of their legal representation, threatening their jobs, and otherwise trying to force them into silence.

The trouble isn't only that cyber-mobs are in control. Treating opinions other than one's own not as differences to be tolerated, but rather as treason to be punished: this is not a legacy of the civil rights movement. At best, it is a descent into rule of the strong, enshrinement of the notion that might makes right.

If Christians were trying to make it harder for legal representatives of abortion rights groups to help their clients, that would be national news. If they were pouring into people's neighborhoods and harassing academics who testify in court, every civil rights organization in America would be denouncing them.

Revisionism did eventually come to Salem Village; it also came during the Red Scare; and it came, relatively swiftly, following the infamous day-care panic of the 1980s. If history is any guide, revisionism will one day come for today's latter-day inquisitors too—leaving future generations to hear of "watchdog groups" and "hate speech" with the same queasiness that many adults today hear the toxic phrase "enemies list." But we are not there yet.

The importance of shaming and cyber-bullying to the securing of ideological victories is also vivid in another realm: secular universities. So chronic are the efforts to establish and police dissent-free zones that it is worth wondering whether today's campuses would even *be* as progressive as they are absent such tactics.

As we saw in chapter 2, challenges to free speech on campuses can be found all over these days; there is enough material in that topic for several books. Just as interesting are the means by which dissent is suppressed—because these reveal much about how universities have become safe places for some people, and menacing places for others.

Exhibit A, from the "city of dreaming spires," as the poet Matthew Arnold called Oxford, England, is a case in which social media mob tactics were used to silence dissent in one of the world's foremost free speech citadels.

In November 2014, a group called Oxford Students for Life scheduled a debate over the proposition of whether abortion was good or bad for Great Britain. It was canceled at the last possible moment. The speakers pro and con—and incidentally volunteering their time—were literally standing on train platforms in London when each got word that the debate was off. Some interesting articles later explored what had happened: a social media storm started by a feminist group frightened away any prospective hosts. The college, it was explained, canceled on account of "security concerns." Milton, Locke, John Stuart Mill and other British defenders of free speech as a paramount right must have flipped in their graves—especially Locke, who is buried at Christchurch College, steps away from where the debate would have taken place.[21]

This illiberal scenario has been repeated over and over on American campuses, to the apparent satisfaction of the people who prosecute these shutdowns, and with little or no objection from others on their side who know such tactics to be wrong.

Consider a couple of recent incidents at another institution of higher learning renowned around the world, Stanford University.

In 2014, a tradition-minded nondenominational student group named for English philosopher Elizabeth Anscombe invited several distinguished speakers to a conference on "marriage, family, and sexual integrity." Progressive activists charged that the conference would feature "hate speech"—whereupon the Graduate Student Council voted to revoke the six hundred dollars in funding that it had previously agreed to.[22] The GSC also attempted to charge the Anscombe Society an extra five thousand dollars in security costs—allegedly because its speakers would "threaten the safety of campus for the queer population."

The head of the Anscombe Society correctly dubbed this a "tax on free speech," and the resulting publicity led Stanford to declare that the society would not have to pay the extra security costs after all—that time around, anyway.

Nonetheless, the Society again became a target in 2015. In announcing its conference for that year, the group went out of its way to stress that this was not a gathering about same-sex marriage or other subjects guaranteed to cause an uproar. It was instead exactly what it purported to be: a discussion of the fallout from the worldwide sexual revolution—a subject about which a wide range of scholars and thinkers have weighed in for decades.

Again, the conference participants would have been judged unobjectionable—by anyone who wasn't prowling the landscape for heretics. The proposed participants included a physician and neurobiologist who previously served on the President's Council on Bioethics; an award-winning sociologist; an economist; a former nurse and founder of an organization to study bioethics; a philosophy professor; the founder of a new think tank; and other distinguished figures whose perspectives might have seemed intrinsically interesting.

The Society's painstaking attempts to explain that the conference was in intellectual earnest made no difference to its detractors, who protested with the usual epithets about "hate speech" and "feeling unsafe." Scores of medical school students and faculty signed a petition asking that the conference be moved. According to the Anscombe Society, "The move was orchestrated by the medical school administration following a petition that threatened a serious protest on the medical school campus during admitted students day if the conference did not move." (Stanford disputed that categorization, chalking up the change to administrative error.)

So far, so familiar; shakedowns and shutdowns of moral traditionalists on campus aren't news, even for nonreligious groups like this one. This probably isn't the first time anyone has wondered how many more conferences the Anscombe Society—or any other dissident student group—will muster before these intimidation tactics finally become prohibitive, and they give up. But the real question we should be asking is this: what could be so frightening about a conference organized to discuss the sexual revolution—unless some people are so metaphysically invested in it that the notion of its being a legitimate subject for discussion is perceived as a gargantuan threat?

It is true, as people following such trends have pointed out, that threats to free speech generally have increased in recent years, especially on campuses. The Foundation for Individual Rights in Education estimates that just under half of the 440 colleges and universities it analyzes maintain policies that "seriously infringe upon the free speech rights of students."[23] In that sense, it may be tempting to chalk up the baiting of groups like the Anscombe Society, and the harassing of scholars like Ryan T. Anderson of the Heritage Foundation, as just two more examples of the trend.

Yet the blind prejudice aimed against traditionalists is unique. If the same systematic, punitive efforts were made to derail speakers from NARAL, or PETA, or such leftist standard-bearers as the

Center for American Progress—#freespeech would be the hottest hashtag in America.

Intimidation is also the bottom line in the harassment and vilification of other heretics who dissent from secularist-progressive orthodoxy.

In 2014, the left-leaning British magazine *New Statesman* ran a cover story by former editor Cristina Odone deploring what she called the "new intolerance" in the United Kingdom.[24] Odone experienced the ugly face of bigotry up close when she attempted to speak at a conference on marriage organized by the legal group Christian Concern, only to find it hastily reshuffled to another venue, twice, when hosts disinvited the speakers. Asking, "Will we regret pushing Christians out of public life?," her essay concludes:

> Let outsiders see the faithful as a vulnerable group persecuted by right-on and politically correct fanatics who don't believe in free speech. Let them see believers pushed to the margins of society, in need of protection to survive. Banned, misrepresented, excluded—and all because of their religion? Even the most hardbitten secularist and the most intolerant liberal should be offended by the kind of censorship people of faith are facing today.

Yesterday's liberals, most of whom considered themselves champions of unfettered belief and expression, would have resonated to that call. Today's secularist-progressive patrolmen do not. Odone's defense of Christians' free speech was excoriated on the left—including by the *New Republic*, once a flagship of American liberalism, which denied that a new wave of "atheistic intolerance" was anything to worry about and called Odone's essay "incoherently argued" and "confusing."[25]

In sum, there's a difference between being persuaded to adopt a new consensus and being frightened away from objecting to it. This is no small difference, either. It's the line separating people ruled by freedom from people ruled by fear. And in the United States today, more and more citizens are being pushed to the wrong side.

5

Inquisitors vs.
Good Works

A few years ago, I met a young woman who spearheads Catholic Charities in one of the archdioceses now under constant legal and public relations siege by progressive activists. Call her Jen. She was every inch a Pope Francis–style Catholic: earnest, self-sacrificing, and pulled closely into the Church's orbit by the gravity of her desire to help society's worst-off people.

Most of her own time and that of like-minded colleagues, Jen lamented, is now spent not where they want to be, in soup kitchens or hospitals or nursing homes or with destitute immigrants. Rather, they must parry constant maneuvers by activists intent on closing down their foster care and adoption services—not because of the contraception mandate, in this case, but for the sole reason that traditional Judeo-Christian teachings about the family infuriate some progressives.

Jen fretted about the work they couldn't accomplish. She worried most of all about the children waiting to be adopted or otherwise brought into a family, those for whom the Church cares as no one else. "I know the time is coming when we'll either close our doors, or decide to keep up our work regardless—in which case we'll end up in jail," this twenty-something woman said matter-of-factly. "But who will take care of the children? Not the people who have sued us out of existence—they'll just move on. Who will take care of all those kids?"

To understand why concerns like these are now front and center among believers, it helps to have some sense of the scope of religious good works. According to PolitiFact, "Catholic charity work is extensive and widely considered a crucial part of the U.S. safety net." Catholic Charities USA alone has more than 2,500 agencies that serve 10 million people annually; moreover, the 18,000 Catholic parishes in the United States spend an average of $200,000 apiece on the needy *beyond* what they give to Catholic Charities and other groups. And these numbers do not begin to capture the charitable "footprint" of many other Christian groups that help people in need, among them hospitals, overseas relief efforts, etc.[1]

The alliance arrayed against traditionalist Christians claims to be on the side of the poor and marginalized. But its soft persecution of those same Christians jeopardizes charities that help the poor and marginalized.

Many people—including many who consider themselves secular and progressive—are almost certainly unaware of one more paradox that has resulted from the collision of secularist orthodoxy and traditionalist Christian ethics: In the name of making the world march in ideological lockstep, the secularist alliance routinely wages legal and public relations war on Christian charities of all kinds—thereby draining resources away from the people whom the charities endeavor to aid.

This is a vital story for two reasons. First is its intrinsic humanitarian dimension. It is impossible to hurt charities that help the poor without hurting the poor.

Second—and critical to understanding the deeper motivations behind the war on religious freedom—is that the story of what's happening to Christian charities affirms the seismic changes in contemporary cultural reality. What best explains the incessant attacks by progressive activists on Christian charities is that the activists are behaving not like rational actors seeking the public good but like quasi-religious zealots. Motivated less by spite and malice, one must assume, than by a doctrine of faith all their own, they are seeking to spread their gospel in the world for its betterment—including to quasi-heathens, that is, Christians who have yet to conform to the commandments of the sexual revolution.

Begin with some facts about what happened, for example, in 2006, when Boston's Catholic Charities was forced to close the adoption agency it had run in that city for 103 years. A new municipal rule would have forced the agency to place children in nontraditional households, meaning those without a married mother and father. Rather than capitulate to progressive demand and thus contradict its church's teaching about the family, Catholic Charities instead closed down its adoption operation.

The result was the loss of an infrastructure that had been integral to adoptions in Boston well beyond the Catholic community. As the *Boston Globe* put it, "The numbers tell a powerful, though partial, piece of the story. Last year, Catholic Charities found more homes for foster children than any other private agency in Massachusetts. . . . In two decades working with DSS [Department of Social Services], Catholic Charities arranged 720 adoptions."[2]

Moreover—to sound what might be called a Burkean point,

named for the philosopher Edmund Burke, about the need to respect organically grown local institutions—the agency had also
served the community more generally as a repository of experience,
connections, and advice. People concerned with child welfare outside the Catholic orbit also benefited from this network and its resources. No more. As the president of the Massachusetts Society for
the Prevention of Cruelty to Children observed at the time, "Catholic Charities has really been a gold standard in providing adoption
services to children in the welfare system for a long time, so this is a
tragedy. This is a tragedy for kids."

Such activist pressure against a Christian agency to capitulate or
close has been repeated around the country. It is one among many
examples of how the quasi-theology of the sexual revolution inter-
feres with religiously inspired efforts to help the poor and destitute,
on several fronts simultaneously: by diminishing or destroying the
institutional knowledge amassed by the organizations under attack;
by draining finite resources out of charities and into prolonged legal
battles; and by siphoning energy and inspiration away from charity
and into skirmishes that suck resources away from good works and
into the courts.

This head-on collision between the commandments of Christianity and the opposing commandments of the sexual revolution
causes collateral damage precisely among those who can least afford
it. Religious leaders have been explaining this for years. Consider
Archbishop Joseph E. Kurtz, president of the United States Conference of Catholic Bishops, at a 2015 meeting of the U.S. bishops: "Let
us pray," he exhorted, that "we don't lose our presence in the public
square to a misguided secularization that reduces faith to the least
common denominator and erodes the very richness of belief that
impels people of faith to serve unselfishly those most in need."[3]

The syllogism is obvious: one can't undercut or close Christians charities, as foot soldiers warring in the name of the sexual revolution want to do, without hurting the people whom the churches help. That's a lot of collateral damage to ask America and the world to accept.

Consider the scope of Catholic charitable work in Philadelphia alone. As Archbishop Charles J. Chaput has written:

> Critics sometimes claim that America's bishops talk too much about issues like abortion and religious freedom while they overlook the poor. . . .
>
> Consider this: In Philadelphia we spend less than $200,000 a year on the archdiocesan office that handles sanctity of life, family and laity issues. It has one full time employee. Most of our specifically "prolife" work is done by volunteers, and at the parish level.
>
> In comparison, we spend more than 4.2 million privately donated archdiocesan dollars each year—every year—on social services for the poor, the homeless, the disabled, troubled youths, battered women, immigration counseling, food pantries and nutritional programs. And we manage another $100 million in public funding for the same or similar efforts. We have 1,600 full time employees spread across these Catholic social ministries doing the works of mercy. . . .
>
> If there's anything "lopsided" about the real witness of the Catholic Church in Philadelphia, it's weighted heavily in favor of the poor. *It always has been.* And that's the reality in nearly every diocese in the United States.[4]

Protestants as well as Catholics testify that progressive efforts to score ideological points clash with their efforts to help the poor. John Ashmen, president of the Protestant evangelical Association of Gospel Rescue Missions, has made the same point as Archbishops Kurtz and Chaput: that ideological battles like the one launched by the contraceptive mandate cannot help but interfere with Christian charity.

All Christians are asking for, he writes, is "freedom to care for the poor"—a freedom that is the more compelling given the scale on which many church-based charities operate. In his mission alone, he notes,

> every agency is full every single night. Last year, our 300 member missions served 66 million restaurant-style meals at no cost and provided 20 million nights of safe shelter. Hundreds of thousands of volunteers and professionals—motivated by their faith—assisted 45,000 adults in finding employment, graduated 16,000 from addiction recovery programs, and placed 36,000 individuals and families into independent housing. Each of the 300 missions stays open 24 hours a day, 365 days a year.[5]

Ashmen also draws attention to one more kind of harm: replacement costs. "Not only do these organizations reduce the burden on American taxpayers" by taking care of people who are otherwise dependent wholly on the state. There is a Burkean point to be made here as well, about the difference between being helped by anonymous state bureaucrats on the one hand—or people animated deeply on account of religion by their desire to help. "The way they serve," he points out, "is with personal touches of love and kindness—touches that they are ideally suited to provide."

Catholic Charities and Gospel Rescue Missions are only two of the many religious charitable organizations caring for millions of needy people inside the United States and out. These works are made possible by a well documented phenomenon that demands to be understood at a time when Christian charities are the objects of destructive litigation: Not only are the charities themselves hard or impossible to replace. So too is the financial reality that makes them possible in the first place: religious believers, including and especially American Christians, give significantly more of their time and money to charities of all kinds than nonbelievers.

So wide is this divide that it has been dubbed "the charity gap" by social scientist Arthur Brooks, whose definitive work on that subject lays out the differences in detail. His analysis, he writes, is "the fruit of years of analysis on the best national and international datasets available on charity, lots of computational horsepower, and the past work of dozens of scholars who have looked at various bits and pieces of the charity puzzle."[6]

Brooks's research shows that religious people give more to charity than nonreligious people—much more: "an enormous charity gap," he reports, "remains between religious and secular people."

> To see this, imagine two women who are both forty-five years old, white, married, have an annual household income of $50,000, and attended about a year of college. The only difference between them is that one goes to church every week, but the other never does. The churchgoing woman will be 21 percentage points more likely to make a charitable gift of money during the year than the non-churchgoer, and she will also be 26 points more likely to volunteer. Furthermore, she will tend to give $1,383 more per year to charity, and to volunteer on 6.4 more occasions.[7]

Brooks goes on to test the charity gap in various dimensions. The results are always the same: the stronger the religious belief and practice, the more is given to charity.

> People who pray every day (whether or not they go to church) are 30 percentage points more likely to give money to charity

than people who never pray (83 to 53 percent). And people saying they devote a "great deal of effort" to their spiritual lives are 42
points more likely to give than those devoting "no effort" (88 to
46 percent). Even a belief in beliefs themselves is associated with
charity. People who say that "beliefs don't matter as long as you're
a good person" are dramatically less likely to give charitably (69 to
86 percent) and to volunteer (32 to 51 percent) than people who
think that beliefs do matter.[8]

It's not all dollars and cents. Brooks reports that religious people
also volunteer more than secular people. They even donate more
blood.[9]

The point of elaborating on this "charity gap" is not to observe
that some people are more generous than others. Rather it is to
ask: how much is too much to demand in the name of the sexual
revolution? Given that there isn't exactly a bidding war outside the
churches to replace any of these charitable institutions, how far can
activists go in crippling them before fair-minded people conclude it
is a moral bridge too far?

Here, once more, high-minded progressivist rhetoric contradicts
the hard reality of what anti-Christian activists are actually doing.
"Our faith teaches us that in the face of suffering, we can't stand idly by,
and that we must be that Good Samaritan," President Obama said at a
prayer breakfast.[10] He and other progressive leaders might want to call
home. The real Good Samaritans of the West are the ones now under
attack in the churches—fighting to keep their work alive in the face
of efforts to force sexual revolution gospel into Christian institutions.

Consider a few more examples of how this clash of creeds plays
out—and who pays for it.

Exhibit A: the Obama administration versus the Little Sisters of
the Poor.

During Pope Francis's widely-celebrated visit to the United States in September 2015, President Obama professed to "stand with you in defense of religious freedom and interfaith dialogue, knowing that people everywhere must be able to live out their faith free from fear and free from intimidation." To call these words audacious given the harm inflicted on Christian charities nationwide by the so-called contraceptive mandate is to understate the case. As one headline neatly captured the point, "Obama Touts Religious Liberty to Pope While Litigating to Force 15 Dioceses to Cooperate in Abortion."[11]

And those dioceses are only the beginning. The absolutist insistence on making employers cover contraception even if it violates their consciences has detonated in pantries, soup kitchens, churches, and courts across the land. It has given rise to more than one hundred lawsuits from religious organizations—thereby forcing resources that could have gone to the deprived and impecunious to be consumed on legal help.[12] It told religious organizations everywhere, in effect, to act in ways that violate their religious beliefs, or pony up heavy fees for failing to comply.

Enter the Little Sisters of the Poor, whose mission could soften even the hardest heart: in settings around the country, they take in the old, the sick, and the dying whom everyone else has thrown out, and live with them as a "family." Even among other people engaged in charity work, the Little Sisters are spoken of in hushed tones, so revered are they and so transparently good is their mission.

Pope Francis himself made a point of meeting with them during his 2015 visit to Washington, D.C.[13] Like all good policies, the visit served a multiplicity of purposes: it signaled moral support to an outstanding Catholic charity at a time when it is beleaguered by state power; it tacitly underlined the theological centrality of Christian teaching to help society's castoffs; and it sent a signal around the world that from the point of view of the leader of a billion believers, religious freedom in the United States should not be threatened or in doubt.

In sum, from a public relations perspective, taking on the Little Sisters should have been the political equivalent of slapping babies.

Yet nothing stopped an American administration animated by secularist progressivism from trying to make the Little Sisters knuckle under to whatever is demanded in the sexual revolution's name. In this case, the demand of a competing secularist dogma is that an institution opposed to contraception for two thousand years must now be forced into being complicit in dispensing a product that the Sisters find immoral. In other cases, like adoption, secularist dogma demands that Catholic agencies either tacitly break with two thousand years of other teaching, about the nature of the family—or else lock their doors.

As a result, the Little Sisters brought a lawsuit against the administration arguing that their refusal to comply with the HHS contraception-and-abortifacients mandate will incur millions of dollars in annual fines—dollars that could otherwise feed, house, and warm the people for whom they care.

Undermining the work of the Little Sisters on behalf of people no one else wants is one of many efforts aimed against Christian charity groups. This brings us to Exhibit B: quite apart from legal drainage over the mandate, Christian charities now face other serious hurdles, thanks to ideologically inspired litigation.

The ACLU, for example, sued one of the largest Catholic hospital chains in the country in 2015—because its doctors do not perform abortions.[14] Never mind that one in eight hospital patients is in a Catholic institution, or that Catholic hospitals are renowned for tending to people who might not otherwise seek medical help and who find them through religious networks.

The ACLU has also sued the United States Conference of Catholic Bishops because shelters operated for children and teen immigrants by the USCCB at the southern border do not offer contraception and abortion.[15] This is a particularly telling example of how far progressive activists will go to interfere with Christian charity. The humanitarian need on that border is immense, and the Church is heavily involved in ameliorating it. The USCCB settles a full quarter of the refugees that come into the United States each year—including for starters some 68,000 children and families whose flight across the southern border in summer 2014 made headline news for weeks.[16]

Reasonable people, regardless of their personal religious beliefs, would likely agree that thwarting this kind of work is the last thing a compassionate human being should want to do. Yet the ACLU and like-minded groups target the bishops anyway—because contraception and abortion are their nonnegotiable imperatives.

Pope Francis has repeatedly decried what he calls "ideological colonization" on the international level, to describe governments and nongovernmental organizations that make humanitarian aid contingent on embracing abortion and contraception.[17] In these and other cases, given the opportunity to choose between humanitarianism on the one hand, and dogmatic purity concerning the sexual revolution on the other, the revolution trumps.

These choices have consequences. In the face of the millions of Syrian refugees seeking shelter, one of the largest migrations in modern times, it is churches that have taken the lead in clothing, feeding, settling, connecting migrants with English classes, and otherwise trying to integrate them into new homelands. It is churches that have asked the Obama administration to increase the number of refugees the United States takes in.[18] Yet it is churches, particularly the Catholic Church's Catholic Charities wings, that are repeatedly the objects of progressive legal sabotage—a seeming paradox to which we will return.

Exhibit C: the National Abortion Rights Action League and like-minded groups have sued pregnancy centers across the country—that is, charitable institutions where desperate women can receive free sonograms and aid and support for having a baby, helping with items ranging from medical care to baby furniture and other everyday needs.[19] NARAL and company have repeatedly sought to impede their work via burdensome ordinances and by other political means.

In conjunction with the attorney general of California, for example, NARAL sponsored legislation passed into law in 2015 that requires the state's crisis pregnancy centers to counsel pregnant women about abortion and contraception—in other words, laws forcing Christians to say things that violate their consciences, with the obvious intention driving religious believers out of the business of helping desperate moms.[20] The fate of these centers is now in the courts.

The gritty ideological drive to reduce practical alternatives to abortion raises questions worth meditating upon, quite apart from anyone's personal opinion on that subject.

Why would anyone want to make life more difficult for women in need who want to have babies? Can't secular progressivism have empathy for women who *don't* choose abortion? If the movement is really pro-choice, what about women who choose to give birth? Or who want dearly to do so, given some material help? Who would work to put diapers and other assistance out of such a woman's reach?

These are not just rhetorical questions. They go to the heart of the argument. Something deeper is afoot than is evident from surface rhetoric about "choice" and being "pro-woman."

Suing charitable institutions that fail to conform to un-Christian or anti-Christian demand also spills across borders. Thus, a Catholic nursing home in Belgium that refused to allow one of its patients to be killed on-site was sued in 2016 by the former resident's family, because they had to move her elsewhere for euthanasia.[21] Quebec already requires religious institutions to participate in euthanasia via arranging for the "safe and timely transfer of the patient to a non-objecting institution," and Canada at large will likely soon follow suit.[22] The legal besieging of Christian adoption agencies for failing to recant Christian beliefs about the family is also international in scope; the last remaining Catholic adoption operation in Great Britain, for example, was shuttered in 2012 following years of legal storming.[23]

Consider Exhibit D. The American Humanist Association's motto is "Good without a God." In the name of making the world safe for atheism, it too sues to interfere with Christian attempts at good works. Consider its recent takedown of an elementary charter school in Colorado: SkyView Academy, of the Douglas County School District in Highlands Ranch, and of another charter school in South Carolina, East Point Academy.

As part of a community service project, children in these schools helped to collect donations and assemble shoe boxes stuffed with hygiene items and gifts to be donated to Operation Christmas Child, an evangelical relief effort that gives impoverished children gifts during the holiday season. And because of that, both schools came to be targeted by the humanists.

Now, reasonable people might just assume that giving hygiene products and toys to people who have none might trump ideological spite against Christians; but some people do not understand the depth of secularist animosity. The atheists argued that the toys were "essentially a bribe, expressly used to pressure desperately poor children living in developing countries to convert to Christianity."[24] And so, faced with the threat of being forced to spend prodigious sums on lawyers, both schools ceased participating in the program.

The reason was the same: financial intimidation via legal warfare. As SkyView put it in an email to parents, "Our school has never endorsed any particular religious view. This decision is based on the importance of protecting our school's program, resources, and reputation, which would be at risk if we chose to engage in this national argument."[25] East Point Academy also stressed that "because we do not want to expend school financial resources defending a lawsuit, we are not going to accept Operation Christmas Child boxes." As for the fallout to the miscreants who meant only to help poor people, the frustration was palpable. "We were shocked. This was a project that was intended with complete good will. That's all this was. It was a project to help other kids in other countries who have less than we do," as the school board president at SkyView told a local news channel.[26]

So intimidation tactics worked again to stop well-meaning people from helping the poor. The American Humanist Association declared victory, adding in a press release, "We hope the school will promote charitable giving by working with an organization that does not promote religion." But was there, in fact, any alternative to reaching the *specific* beneficiaries of that evangelical charity?

Once more the Burkean point deserves to be aired: the organically grown, intricate, transnational networks built by Christians and their charities in the course of years, decades, and even centuries are not replaceable—not overnight, not a hundred years from now, and certainly not by government bureaucracies.

If Christianity were to be litigated or otherwise forced out of existence tomorrow, so would its global ties to hundreds of millions of people, in countries across the planet—interconnected, invisible platoons now spanning whole countries and civilizations, as well as the vast majority of languages on earth. How is disrupting these supply lines remotely in the public interest of humanity—or more to the point, in the interests of individual needy human beings whom the charities help?

When your goal in life is to prevent other people from putting toys and soap into the hands of needy children, some deep motive has to be at work. When the purpose of your existence is to shut down an agency that helps children without parents find a loving home, the same thing has got to be true.

What begs for understanding too is that the new secularist pressure on Western Christians makes it harder to help people anywhere else. Financially, politically, and logistically, churches are now forced to play defense against multiple adversaries whose shared purpose is to diminish the influence of Christianity on public life. Institutions that are fighting to keep their operations alive despite legal and other conflicts are at an obvious disadvantage when it comes to helping people elsewhere—for starters, their persecuted brethren in the Middle East. Not that this stops churches from attempting the task. But like oxygen masks on airplanes, their resources must first be used to keep themselves from going under.

Second: the variety of secularist progressivism governing from the White House for two presidential terms has systematically attempted to re-write the permissible scope of action for American Christians, beginning though not ending with the administration's well-documented refusal to speak of "freedom of religion" and its concomitant substitution of the far more restrictive "freedom of worship." As writer Ashley Samelson McGuire has summarized of that shift,

> both President Obama and Secretary of State Hillary Clinton have been caught using the phrase "freedom of worship" in prominent

speeches, rather than the "freedom of religion" the President called for in Cairo. . . . If the swap-out occurred only once or twice, one might appropriately conclude it was merely a rhetorical accident. However, both the President and his Secretary of State have now replaced "freedom of religion" with "freedom of worship" too many times to seem inadvertent. . . . To anyone who closely follows prominent discussion of religious freedom in the diplomatic and political arena, this linguistic shift is troubling.[27]

An ideology that sees Christian public expression as a problem to be reined in at home is unlikely to put the persecution of Christians elsewhere in the world at the top of the to-do list. At a minimum, activists who are gratified by the routs of American Christian traditionalists are unlikely sources of support for people suffering in other countries for that same faith.

In contests pitting the abject and downtrodden against the demands of secularist writ, the abject and downtrodden lose. If the poor can't be made to serve the sexual revolution, the thinking seems to run, to hell with them.

A few years ago, a national leader on behalf of same-sex marriage, Jonathan Rauch, observed that "[i]f Catholic Charities doesn't want to place children for adoption with same-sex couples in Massachusetts but lots of other agencies will make the placement, we can live with that."[28] That reasonable idea—of religious citizens and their adversaries working together toward the common good of people beside themselves, even as they acknowledge their differences—has been sounded almost nowhere else on his side of the discussion.

Deep credal passions are at work here—and not just those of Christians. Otherwise, why would other people work so hard to

accomplish goals that on the face of things are inexplicable and hurt-
ful, like harassing and even closing charities that help poor people?

The answer is that they do not think what they do is deplorable.
They believe they are in possession of a higher truth, and they fight
to universalize it—to proselytize just as anyone else who believes
himself charged with guardianship of the Truth seeks to do.

Beneath the clashes over Christian charities lies a massive tec-
tonic shift in Western cultures generally. Whether you believe that
Jesus Christ was the Son of God on earth, or believe instead that this
story is the greatest lie that gullible humanity has ever been told,
is immaterial. Surely, seeing the vehemence with which Christian
charities are now attacked, people of reason can agree: the so-called
culture wars are not about libertarian freedom versus religious un-
freedom. They're about a conflict between two rival faiths.

The story of the charities and why they are now under fire is
not simply one of humanitarian consequence. It is also confirma-
tion that in this cultural theater, as in others, two orthodoxies—
summoning all the fealty and determination that only orthodoxies
can—now compete. A new form of (mostly though not always) non-
violent religious war has been born between one group of believers
following a creed whose outlines appeared two thousand years ago
and an opposed group of believers following a secularist creed that
has developed in the last half century following the technological
shock of the Pill.

How they are ever to live together is among the most compelling
questions in the West today.

6

What Is to Be Done; or,
How to End a Witch Hunt

In 2014, Home and Garden Television (HGTV) canceled a planned reality show in which twin brothers and former star baseball players David and Jason Benham, from North Carolina, were to fix up properties and help people to buy homes. The day before the show's cancellation, a report had been posted by Right Wing Watch denouncing the brothers as pro-life, Christian sons of a Christian family—in particular emphasizing their evangelical pastor father, who had spoken in defense of traditional biblical teachings.[1]

Like many other Christians now on the receiving end of intolerance for transgressing the new secularist orthodoxy, the brothers professed shock and denied any wrongdoing. "[W]e've sold thousands of homes with the guiding principle of producing value and breathing life into each family that has crossed our path," they said in a statement, "and we do not, nor will we ever discriminate against people who do not share our views." In another statement, they added: "If our faith costs us a TV show, so be it."[2]

My faith vs. my job.
My faith vs. my social standing.
My faith vs. my future.

For more and more Christians, such either-or thought experiments aren't theoretical exercises. They are constant real-life companions.

A few years into the third millennium, in a transformation that has taken almost everyone by surprise, these believers have gone from being mainstays of Western culture to existential question marks within it. They risk public vitriol and endure penalties against which other groups are protected, and the venues and institutions through which their beliefs and ideas are transmitted have become objects of unique assault. On account of these developments, their future—and with it the future of religious freedom itself—appears more clouded than at any time since the American founding.

How can we get out of this punitive place?

One answer, extrapolated from current realities, is that escape is no longer an option. Maybe today's people of faith will live to see their beliefs increasingly vilified, their charities strangled by litigation, their children ostracized, their social standing further reduced, their commercial possibilities circumscribed, their faith forced into the closet, and their religious institutions either compromised or financially kneecapped. Many religious believers already suspect this trajectory to be under way, which is why some now debate a "Benedict option" for withdrawing from the world. Such is one prospective Western tomorrow.

But there is another possibility—perhaps less likely, but more elevating. The path to a more magnanimous place begins with an understanding that there is a new dynamic between believers and everyone else, in this new sequel to the culture war, and that the actions to be taken depend on seeing that dynamic clearly.

What's unfolding today is not a drama in which secularist progressivism is slowly but surely eclipsing antiquated religious faith at last, but a contest of competing creeds, and competing first principles. Only when we acknowledge that truth can we see that there is only one way out of this cantankerous, riven place.

We need to understand that there's a new faith in Western civilization: a quasi-religious faith in the developing secularist catechism about the sexual revolution. Believers in secularist orthodoxy can either follow the Puritans in Massachusetts, punishing the stray Baptists and Quakers and others who find themselves in their midst, or they can opt for what Thomas Jefferson and other Founders developed as an antidote to Puritan destructiveness, namely, the shared understanding that one's own liberty isn't safe until everyone else's is protected.

About matters concerning the sexual revolution, in other words, as about other articles of deeply held faith, people must agree to disagree. That is the sine qua non of a more civil tomorrow.

We can also look to the lessons of preceding moral panics. As it happens, both Salem and McCarthyism offer similar blueprints that point the way out. In both cases, resolution demanded that people hitherto silent take a stand in the name of the public good.

In the case of Salem, two developments were needed to bring an end to the witch trials. One was a change in the admissibility of certain kinds of evidence that had been used to charge people with being a "witch." "Spectral" evidence—that is, "evidence" that was not empirically verifiable—was ruled out. That is how the witch hunters were ultimately disarmed: by being deprived of evidence that others could not verify for determining who was a "witch."

The second force was a collective moral awakening. Persecutors and their fellow travelers came slowly, but consequentially, to perceive the human reality before them. No longer did they reflexively see putative witches as dehumanized, cartoonish villains responsible for all manner of alleged transgressions. Instead, the falsely accused were recognized once more as neighbors and friends, family members and fellow citizens, who had been wrongfully caught up in a social panic. The people of Salem absorbed the damage the witch hunt had caused, and came to agree, as the influential Rev. Increase Mather put it, that "it was better to let ten suspected witches go free than one innocent person be condemned."[3]

Both of these changes—a banning of the equivalent of spectral evidence, and a collective awakening about what unbridled activism has been committing against Christians in the name of progressivism—are needed now not only in Salem and the rest of the United States, but across the Western world.

Symmetrical lessons can be found in the dénouement of the Red Scare of the 1950s. What put an end to McCarthyism was a realignment of opinion among people who slowly but surely decided that they did not want to be party to the injustices being committed against some of their neighbors.

"We must not confuse dissent with disloyalty. We must remember always that accusation is not proof," as journalist Edward R. Murrow summarized this understanding. It was Murrow's documentary exposing some of McCarthy's groundless charges that dealt a blow from which the senator never recovered. But it was the actions of people on McCarthy's own side that were decisive—those of the political right who disassociated themselves from his bullying tactics, beginning with seven Republican senators.

All of which is to say that neither the accused witches of Salem nor the objects of the Red Scare were able to end those moral panics on their own. Momentum for change had to come from the other side. The same is true of the present antagonism toward religious citizens. What's needed is for people on the other side to acknowledge that things have gone too far.

The rhetorical question that put the final nail in McCarthyism, posed by army counsel Joseph Welch and famously repeated ever since, was "Have you no decency, sir?" An analogous appeal to decency is now required in the riven societies of the West, if the believers are to be treated once more as the social and moral equals of secularists and progressives, rather than as latter-day witches inflicting spectral harm.

Alongside that comes some practical corollaries. The promiscuous hurling of the terms *hater* and *-phobe* is one example. These have become words used to smear, shame, and silence, not elucidate or clarify. Like a Trojan horse, they express the idea that there can be no rational or principled basis for opposing any particulars of the political agenda set forth by people who deploy those terms; all such opposition, their use implies, can only come from prejudice and fear.

Words used to bar other people from a place at the human table are words that are worth thinking twice about.

People outside the ranks of the believers might also lean in toward civility by trying to understand where their religious neighbors are coming from. Christian regulation of sexual mores is not something new under the sun, cooked up simply for the nefarious purpose of obstructing the civil rights of enlightened people who reject all that. Nor is it a reflection of prejudice, fear, or a desire to repress natural impulses in ourselves and others.

From its earliest days, Christianity declared that a wide number of behaviors common to Roman civilization were off-limits for the followers of Jesus Christ. These included contraception, infanticide,

divorce, bestiality, and all forms of nonmarital sex.[4] This traditionalist moral code proved a hard sell to many people even as it held
an irresistible appeal for many others. Across history, the code has
been reviled, resisted, and complained about—beginning with the
disciples themselves, whose first response when told by Jesus that
divorce will now be off-limits is to object that this is a "hard teaching." At the same time, it has drawn other people into the Church,
including some of the most effective converts across the centuries.
The point is that the code has endured minority status before, and
is enduring it again. Like the Judaism from which it sprang, Christianity has been defined in part precisely by the rules that set it apart
from other faiths.

And that consistency is exactly the point: because up until now
in the free societies of the West—thanks in no small part to the genius of the American Founders—non-Christians, and even anti-
Christians, have generally allowed their neighbors to hold this set
of beliefs without ostracizing them for it. And therein lies another
key to the way out.

Nowhere today are practicing Christians called "contracepto-
phobes"—even though two thousand years of consistent teaching
have proscribed contraception, and even though Western Christians have long lived in societies where it is ubiquitous. To the contrary: their neighbors who disagree with them have for the most
part decided to live and let live about that difference (until Obamacare, anyway).

Similarly: nowhere are Christian believers called "divorce-
ophobes," "infanticide-ophobes," or "bestiality-ophobes"—though
their traditionalist moral code says no to these behaviors as well.
They are not even called "aborto-phobes"—this despite the fact that
abortion remains one of the most contentious issues in the Western world. Nor are they dismissed as "polygamy-phobes" (at least,

not yet). If those epithets have no traction as slurs, others shouldn't either. Citing Judeo-Christian teachings about marriage as "proof" that believers "hate" anybody is the modern equivalent of using spectral evidence to convict witches: it does not prove what it claims to prove.

"Christian bigot"—another phrase that rolls trippingly off some tongue these days—ought to take its place alongside other labels used to isolate and marginalize. "Theocrat" is another epithet empty of content apart from being used to impugn motive. The *Oxford English Dictionary* defines *theocracy* as "A form of government in which God (or a deity) is recognized as the king or immediate ruler, and his laws are taken as the statute-book of the kingdom, these laws being usually administered by a priestly order as his ministers and agents; hence (loosely) a system of government by a sacerdotal order, claiming a divine commission; also, a state so governed."

Until and unless a political movement is launched to replace the United States Constitution with the Bible, or the Magna Carta with the book of Deuteronomy, "theocrat" should be seen for what it is: one more emotionally charged word deployed against believers to prevent open discussion. A little more mindfulness about language might help a lot toward an overdue awakening of civility.

Similarly, the intimidation and exiling of supposed heretics who disagree with some or all of progressivism's dogmatic particulars about the sexual revolution needs to stop. If it's wrong to circulate posters of abortionists with words like *murderer* at the top, then it's equally wrong to incite passion by calling religious people "haters."

Reasonable people of a-religious or even anti-religious inclination might also err on the side of magnanimity by acknowledging the possibility that believers have something to offer the wider society—including not only their charitable operations, but also their expanding critique of a revolution that continues to transform the whole world. Just as the fifty-plus years since the invention of the birth control pill have resulted in a well-developed and intricately connected secularist-progressive body of thought, so have those years given rise to an opposing critique from the believers' side—one focused not on the sexual revolution's empowerments, but rather on its arguably under-attended downside, especially its effects on society's smaller and weaker members. This contrarian set of arguments, too, deserves a respectful public hearing.

As scholars have been pointing out for years—including scholars with no religious agenda at all—the poor are the canaries in the coal mines of the sexual revolution. Consider new evidence from sociologist W. Bradford Wilcox and Robert I. Lerman's recent work, *For Richer, for Poorer: How Family Structures Economic Success in America*. Among the findings:

> We estimate that the growth in median income of families with children would be 44 percent higher if the United States enjoyed 1980 levels of married parenthood today. Further, at least 32 percent of the growth in family-income inequality since 1979 among families with children and 37 percent of the decline in men's employment rates during that time can be linked to the decreasing number of Americans who form and maintain stable, married families.[5]

The sexual revolution, in other words, has been driving one of the most divisive political issues in Western society today: income inequality. It has been driving the middle class into the ground. And that is only the beginning of the problems presented by some of the revolution's unforeseen consequences.

Christians don't deserve to be cast out of a community whose shared concerns outweigh its differences. For example, it is not only religious folk who worry over another vital microcosm these days: American campuses. Just over a decade ago, Tom Wolfe published his dark classic, *I Am Charlotte Simmons*—demonstrating in excruciating detail the journey of a modern Everygirl at an elite college. Harrowing memoirs now abound of sexual assault, drunken coercion, date-rape drugs, and other depredations cataloged there.

That reality is one more reason for ceasing and desisting secular-progressive attacks on Christian schools. Put aside questions about free exercise and free speech. For millions of parents and students, religious higher education matters above all for this reason: because it stands as an alternative to the predatory pandemonium found on many secular campuses.

As one journalist captured the difference between her own secular college and her sister's Christian one:

> The posters on the walls in my all-female freshman dorm at Tufts offered information about eating disorders, what to do if you think you have been sexually assaulted, and suicide and depression hotlines. The Hillsdale walls that I saw were covered with advertisements for quilting clubs, charity opportunities and a listing of local churches.[6]

Similarly, when a young female student was murdered at the University of Virginia in 2010 by her sometime boyfriend, a student at the Christian college Patrick Henry observed that the past four years had seen no violent crime at his own school, leading to this reflection:

> Critics mock us for our strict rules like no dancing or drinking on campus, no members of the opposite sex permitted in your dorm room, nightly curfew hours. . . . We have been the subject

of books (*God's Harvard*), television shows, op-eds, and count-
less blogs who rant against our brand of overbearing right-wing
Christianity that poisons society's freedom. Yet, what is the cost
of students being able to "express" themselves? Is that freedom
worth the cost of drunk driving deaths, drug related violence, and
love affairs turned fatal?[7]

Maybe the believers' countercultural experiences and institutional practices might be of interest to administrators who now
wonder how to make secular schools safer for women without
torpedoing the civil rights of men. After all, people from all over
sometimes find themselves wanting to draw a line *somewhere* on the
sexual revolution—especially if they are parents. Damon Linker, for
example, observed of the phenomenon of Tinder that

> Baby Boomers or Gen-Xers (like myself)—will find this vision of
> dating as a series of technologically facilitated one-off hook-ups
> with near-strangers to be pretty appalling. I know I do. There's just
> one problem: In order for this reaction to amount to more than
> an old fogey's sub-rational expression of disgust at the behavior of
> the young, it has to make reference to precisely the kind of elabo-
> rate account of morality—including binding standards of human
> flourishing and degradation—that liberals have worked to jetti-
> son, in the name of sexual liberation, for the past half-century.[8]

The believers also have a perspective worth weighing in their
other concerns over the revolution's fallout. Surely devotees of the
Bible are not the *only* people to suspect that there might be a problem in the fact that millions more girls are aborted than boys. It
is similarly empirical fact that unborn black babies are far more
likely to be aborted than are white ones. Can't people who sincerely

believe that statistics like these may be evidence of injustice make their case outside the religious ghetto, rather than frog-marched toward the gibbet?

Surely some can get a mainstream hearing when they point with concern toward, say, trial balloons for "post-birth" abortion, that is, efforts to legalize the killing of unwanted infants. One needn't wear a bracelet asking "What Would Jesus Do?" to wonder about the wisdom of okaying infanticide, or to see that the so-called "slippery slope" leading up to that position is no fiction of the religious imagination, but public fact. The prestigious *Journal of Medical Ethics* devoted an entire issue to discussion of infanticide in 2013, centered on a previously published article arguing that "after-birth abortion (killing a newborn) should be permissible in all the cases where abortion is, including cases where the newborn is not disabled."[9] Within academia, infanticide has been considered a respectable subject of discussion for many years now, including though not only within philosophical circles dominated by utilitarianism.[10] Debate about whether these thought experiments amount to moral progress shouldn't be out of bounds, either.

Now that *Obergefell v. Hodges* has settled the legal status of same-sex marriage, there may be hope of resuming a wider conversation about other issues affecting the whole of society and the kind of place the Western world wants to be—one in which religious views are heard with respect, rather than gagged by online bailiffs or ignored because they are Christian. It's a conversation that's needed for reasons also worth consideration.

First, the question of the sexual revolution and its fallout isn't just some boutique preoccupation of the faithful. It doesn't take a card-carrying theist to question what's going on out there in the post-Pill world.

For starters, the consequences of the revolution have been

mapped over the decades by people without any religious agenda. Walter Lippmann—not exactly a Christian standard-bearer—argued that the use of contraception would change the world.[11] Pitirim Sorokin, founder of Harvard University's department of sociology, critiqued the sexual revolution in terms that would have had him in handcuffs in some places today, and denied tenure just about everywhere.[12] The bigotry that now shouts down social scientists and other researchers who reach unwanted conclusions about newly popular articles of faith would shout down a long list of others, including the likes of contrarian social theorists such as Lionel Tiger, Kay Hymowitz, the late Daniel Patrick Moynihan, George Gilder, Charles Murray, Judith Wallerstein, and other honest researchers sifting through data for empirical truth. Is the censorship of independent minds really to be progressivism's historical signature?

It stands to reason, after all, that one of the most consequential developments in human history, the technological separation of recreation from procreation, would have aftershocks for centuries to come, and that curious minds would want to trace them.

French novelist Michel Houellebecq, for example, has become to the sexual revolution what Charles Dickens was to the industrial revolution of the 1800s: its fictional chronicler of first resort. And Houellebecq's vision is dystopian. As his narrator notes in *The Elementary Particles*, the novel that first catapulted its author to international acclaim:

It is interesting to note that the "sexual revolution" was sometimes portrayed as a communal utopia, whereas in fact it was simply another stage in the historical rise of individualism. As the lovely word "household" suggests, the couple and the family would be the last bastion of primitive communism in liberal society. The sexual revolution was to destroy these intermediary communities, the last to separate the individual from the market. The destruction continues to this day.[13]

By the standards of secularist progressive quasi-theology, this critique amounts to heresy, even though—or maybe especially because—it comes from an author with no ostensible religious agenda at all. Yet there is bound to be much more revisionism in the future, as other social observers drawn by the gravity of the revolution's impact comb the same gigantic fallout and rethink.

The novels of English writer Martin Amis return to the revolution repeatedly. His 2010 fiction *The Pregnant Widow* is a full-scale meditation on what the post-Pill world has wrought. "[T]he revolution was a velvet revolution," his narrator explains at the end, "but it wasn't bloodless; some came through, some more or less came through, and some went under."[14] If it's all right for literary men of the left to open up this subject for discussion, then it should be all right for other people to air revisionist thoughts, too.

One shouldn't risk social banishment, for example, by asking how some of the novel human experiments conducted today might look in history's rearview mirror. It's legitimate to wonder whether there are things that shouldn't be bought, sold, or rented. In 2012, in India—then the world capital for paid commercial surrogacy—a woman orphaned her own two children when she died in childbirth, serving as a paid surrogate to wealthy Westerners.[15] In 2014, in what is known as the "Baby Gammy" case, an Australian couple who paid a surrogate mother in Thailand rejected the consequent baby born with Down syndrome, and took that baby's twin home instead.[16] To wonder whether there might be something wrong with those pictures shouldn't invite penalty.

The sexual revolution today has its cheerleaders, its style pages, its movies, and its laws. It does not yet have, or perhaps is only beginning to get, its William Hogarths, its Charles Dickenses, its Jonathan Swifts, its Martin Luther King Jrs. Yet there are signs that the status quo ante may be changing.

In response to the Baby Gammy case, for example, feminists in different countries made common cause with traditionalists in opposing surrogacy as inimical to human well-being; and in 2012, a board member of the National Organization for Women (NOW), Kathy Sloan, was a prominent voice arguing against the legalization of commercial surrogacy in New Jersey; Governor Chris Christie subsequently vetoed the bill in question.[17] The material for questioning some of what's happening out there abounds already, and one suspects more realignment to come. The mounting critique of some of the revolution's experiments is one that open-minded people should make room for, because it concerns momentous facts.

Second, people outside churchgoing circles might understand that the same revolution has given rise to the cultural equivalent of counterrevolutionaries—people who are persuaded toward religion itself, and act upon their convictions. Sooner or later, secularist progressives are going to have to find some way to live with those voluntary dissenters. They include some who see themselves as former victims of the battles, the walking wounded coming in and out of those proverbial "field hospitals" about which Pope Francis has spoken: women who regret their abortions, people who consciously forsake secularist beliefs behind for religious ones, and men and women who for reasons of their own demur about various chapters or verses in the new secularist catechism.

This itinerant but continuous exodus out of non-religious territories and into religious ones is ecumenical—neither just a Catholic nor a Protestant thing. As Russell D. Moore observes in his 2015 book *Onward: Engaging the Culture without Losing the Gospel,*

> The sexual revolution cannot keep its promises. People think
> they want autonomy and transgression, but what they really want is
> fidelity and complementarity and incarnational love. If that's true,
> then we will see a wave of refugees from the sexual revolution.[18]

We're already seeing it. These are the true contrarians of our time—the believers who do not want to jettison the Judeo-Christian moral code, but want to do something more radical: namely, live by it.

Whether cradle Christians or deathbed converts, all of these people deserve the courtesy of recognizing that what they do is authentic, and is being undertaken for reasons of authentic belief— not, as is often insinuated, that they aren't thinking for themselves; or that they're driven by mindless animus; or that they're the dupes of wicked leaders who find them "easy to command"; or other familiar caricatures. If people can abandon traditionalist precincts for progressive ones, religion for irreligion, or old sexual mores for new ones, then the reverse must also apply: conversion and deconversion are two-way streets—and converts to the nonprogressive side don't deserve to be treated as traitors.

As Robert P. George, chairman of the United States Commission on International Religious Freedom, has explained, "the right to religious freedom by its very nature includes the right to leave a religious community whose convictions one no longer shares and the right to join a different community of faith, if that is where one's conscience leads."[19]

Christianity is being built more and more by these witnesses— by people who have come to embrace the difficult, long-standing rulebook not because they know nothing of the revolution and its fallout, but because they know too much. They're the heirs to

St. Augustine and every other soul who ever found in Christianity's tough code a lifesaver, and not a noose. What's more, they aren't going away.[20]

Third, in addition to the fact that ridding the world of religion is impossible—particularly at a time when the sexual revolution is creating a new generation of converts and counterrevolutionaries of its own, even as it also draws some formerly religious people toward secularist progressivism—there's another fact against the exercise. Ridding the human patrimony of Judeo-Christian art and ideas is a potentially catastrophic exercise in social amnesia.

Leaders within the secular progressive alliance claim the imprimatur of history. But in trying to exorcise Christianity from the public square, these new high priests transgress historical reality and run the risk of robbing future generations of many of humanity's greatest treasures, intellectual and otherwise.

This is the deeper problem with deciding that select verses in Leviticus or Acts are grounds for censure, shaming, and possibly a spell in jail. How long will it be until the writings of Thomas Aquinas are banned for contributing to "hate speech"? Or Pope John Paul II's phenomenological work on "theology of the body"? Or the speeches of Jonathan Edwards, or other great Christian preachers? How long before all of philosophy and theology is thrown on the book pyre, in the name of being on "the right side of history"? Even if wholesale censorship of that tradition were possible, more would always be needed. As we have already seen, the revolution is only beginning to attract the literary attention it deserves.

Secularist progressivism must find a way to coexist with affronts to its own orthodoxy, not suppress them. Across Europe, for example, the political and social scramble to dissociate from the Christian past has reached proportions so unreasonable that it has been dubbed "Christophobia" by Jewish scholar J. H. H. Weiler.[21]

American sociologists George Yancey and David A. Williamson have lately assembled extensive data about prejudice against traditional believers in a study called *So Many Christians, So Few Lions: Is There Christianophobia in the United States?*[22] These are examples of a countercultural literature that is only just beginning to turn the tables on secularism—just as the new atheism put theists in the petri dish, only with the roles reversed.

Europe may be increasingly secular. Even so, it is the treasures of its past that draw pilgrims to the Continent in the first place, secular and religious alike. From Notre Dame to Westminster Abbey, the Sistine Chapel to the Duomo of Florence, Amiens to Chartres to Rouen to Barcelona, from the Borghese Gallery to the Prado to the British Museum, artifacts created to honor God remain centers of cultural gravity. As the Marxist Terry Eagleton rebuked certain new atheists for what he saw as their intellectual vandalism of Christianity, "critics of the richest, most enduring form of popular culture in human history have a moral obligation to confront that case at its most persuasive, rather than grabbing themselves a victory on the cheap by savaging it as so much garbage and gobbledygook."[23]

Attempts to wipe the slate clean of Christianity risk depriving the West of its own intellectual, as well as aesthetic, birthright. A few years ago, for example, under pressure by an atheist group, the U.S. Air Force suspended a course in just-war theory that had been taught for twenty years to officers at Vandenberg Air Force Base, in California—the only place in the United States from which intercontinental ballistic missiles and certain space satellites can be launched.[24]

Like much else in the Judeo-Christian scholastic tradition, just-war theory has been around far longer than the United States itself. It is a body of philosophical thought dedicated to the conditions of justifiable conflict, developed in scholastic detail from Augustine of

Hippo to Thomas Aquinas's systematic exegesis in the 1200s, and running through centuries of other commentary up to the present day.[25] In banning the course, the Air Force promised to look into non-religious "alternatives." Yet there *is* no secular equivalent of just-war theory—any more than there is a secular equivalent of Palestrina; or Renaissance biblical paintings; or iconography; or Gothic cathedral design; or other philosophical and artistic creations left behind by believers across Western history.

Like other intricately developed artifacts and traditions and achievements dedicated to the name of God over millennia, these cannot be replicated. When military officers who can launch missiles capable of killing millions are deprived of the insights of centuries of ethical reasoning on the subject of war, who benefits?

One can't drive religion out of the secularist temple without torpedoing the human patrimony itself. In his recent book *A Deeper Vision: The Catholic Intellectual Tradition in the Twentieth Century*, for example, scholar Robert Royal delivers more than six hundred pages examining the influence of Catholic thinkers and artists on those hundred years alone, including though not limited to such titanic figures as Jacques Maritain, Bernard Lonergan, Josef Pieper, Edith Stein, Romano Guardini, Karl Rahner, Henri du Lubac, Charles Péguy, Paul Claudel, François Mauriac, G. K. Chesterton, Gerard Manley Hopkins, Graham Greene, J. R. R. Tolkien, Czeslaw Milosz, Christopher Dawson, and many more.[26] It is a list that includes many of the most celebrated and influential intellectuals, novelists, playwrights, philosophers, historians, critics, and poets of the past hundred-plus years. As Catholic writer Joseph Bottum has put it, "With two thousand years of history behind it, Catholic thought remains the largest and most elaborate intellectual project the world has ever known, dwarfing all the other systems, from

Confucianism to Marxism, that get called scholasticisms by analogy to their Catholic exemplar." [27]

One more thought might be weighed in this context. Even in secularized Europe, the next chapter in the story of continental Christianity remains unclear; to repeat, historicism doesn't write the script. As author and papal biographer George Weigel has observed in his searching 2005 meditation, *The Cube and the Cathedral: Europe, America, and Politics Without God*:

> [Even in Europe] the picture is not monochromatic, nor is the story line necessarily that of a one-way street leading to a dead end. . . . Modern European history can also be read from another angle, as a history of missionaries, saints, statesmen, men and women of genius, and martyrs—a history of great spiritual dynamism amid rapidly advancing secularization. [28]

In sum, secularist progressivism faces insurmountable obstacles to its desire to impose its orthodoxy on everyone else. There is too much heterodoxy afoot—too many people all over the place who question and dissent. Too much has been accomplished in the name of *religious* orthodoxy to wipe the horizon clean of the thing. Too many of humanity's treasures are risked by the wrecking ball of secularist antagonism. Finally, religious revival and renascence remain viable future bets, as they always have. They cannot be willed away by nouveau historicist decree.

There is no way around it: secularist progressivism must find what it has so far resisted, which is a way of living with the believers without exiling them as heretics or ignoring what they have to say in the hope that they will someday, somehow, become mere petrified artifacts of capital-*H* History.

•   •   •

That's no small "ask" to put forward. For starters, condescension to-ward certain religious believers is long-standing across the Western world, and runs deep. Long before some of the new atheists turned belittling believers into bestselling entertainment, other opponents of organized religion got there first. This is one more obstacle to future comity that has to be countenanced.

Voltaire called Christianity "the most ridiculous, the most absurd and bloodiest religion that has ever infected the world." Friedrich Nietzsche likened the followers of Christ to slaves. Karl Marx com-pared them to opium-eaters. Bertrand Russell declared that "fear is the basis of the whole thing." Long-standing reluctance to grant believers equal intellectual status in the first place is another im-pediment to opening a new conversation: the one needed between people who believe in the commandments of the Bible, and people who believe in the commandments set down by a newer orthodoxy.

By Aristotle's rules, "A" and "Not-A" can't both be true simulta-neously. Between the contradictory claims of traditionalist religion on the one hand and secularist writ on the other, someone is right— and the other party is wrong. The only way to have civil discourse when first principles conflict is to allow that whichever party is wrong . . . is entitled to be wrong.

As Kevin J. "Seamus" Hasson, founder of the Becket Fund for Religious Liberty, which represents religious-liberty plaintiffs of all faiths, has put it well:

> recognizing others' right to be wrong on the ultimate questions
> of life is inconvenient and expensive. But all the other alternatives
> are worse. Repression of religion, whether in the name of an offi-
> cial faith or of an official secularism, doesn't work. It merely builds
> up social pressure and postpones the day when it will vent.[29]

Hasson's point is critical. Generally speaking, humanity is theo-tropic, leaning toward God—or toward gods and idols in some form. The desire of today's anti-theists to turn that wall of separation into a tomb is not only wrong because of what it does to their fellow citizens in purportedly open societies. It's wrong because even without that damage, the effort to wipe away the religious horizon with a sponge—to cite Nietzsche's potent image in his parable about the madman declaring "God is dead"—won't work, as history has repeatedly shown.

Every age turns out people who follow their God, and who insist on listening to what they call "conscience"—even when acting on their beliefs runs against their self-interest, or what their supposedly "selfish" genes ought to be telling them to do. Sooner or later, the unbelievers among them will simply have to get used to it. It takes violence to separate the faithful from their gods, as the history of communism and Nazism amply shows.[30] Other entries in the human ledger demonstrate the same, whether in the story of Shadrach, Meshach, and Abednego in the fire of Nebuchadnezzer; or in the martyrs whose toll can be seen running through the twenty centuries of Christianity. Of the first 32 popes beginning with Peter, 32 were martyred—every one until AD 314.[31] That's another way to measure the persistence of theo-tropism: the fact that in every age, people die for it.

Hasson, following Thomas Jefferson, is right: acknowledging that we all have "the right to be wrong" is the only way out of the fundamental issues posed by the diversity of humanity itself, including its diversity of beliefs; and above all by the apparently ineradicable search for transcendent creeds of *some* sort—including the new secularist one.

All of which raises questions for devotees of the rival faith whose activists now set their faces so resolutely against traditional

Christianity. If, as most of those new followers seem to believe, religion amounts to so many tall tales that most of humanity unfathomably embraces, why not just decide to live and let live? If you don't believe in hell anyway, does it really matter if other people think you might end up there? Protestant fundamentalists may be skeptics about Darwinian theories of evolution, but they aren't dismantling other people's educational institutions or preventing people who think differently from educating their children as they wish. Might not non-theists extend the same courtesy to Christian colleges and homeschoolers?

The political model that points a way out for progressives and traditionalists alike has been there all along: Thomas Jefferson. Complicated as the question of his personal religious views may be, the intellectual and moral foundations of the American experiment are not. The Judeo-Christian roots of the most salient documents of this country's history run deep. As philosopher Michael Novak has written, affirming the reasoning of French Catholic philosopher Jacques Maritain:

> Apart from Christian conceptions of a Creator who asks to be worshiped in spirit and truth, and a Christian conception of the inner forum of inalienable conscience, George Mason's *Virginia Declaration of Rights*, Jefferson's *Bill for Establishing Religious Freedom*, and Madison's *Memorial and Remonstrance* would lose all cogency and sense. These documents owe their derivation to a Jewish and Christian worldview, and do not spring from any other.[32]

Similarly, in their 2014 book *Doubting Thomas? The Religious Life and Legacy of Thomas Jefferson*, Mark A. Beliles and Jerry Newcombe analyze more than one thousand primary documents to conclude that Jefferson was far more involved in religious doings than is commonly supposed.[33] Jefferson studied the New Testament in Greek, attended church, including while in government, had positive relationships with hundreds of clergymen and laymen, and above all, he authored the Virginia Statute for Religious Freedom and thereby created the model for the most important formulation on religious liberty in human history: the First Amendment to the Bill of Rights.

Even if Jefferson's participation in organized religion were purely cynical, as some scholars have argued, such opportunism does not undercut the fact that his "wall of separation" metaphor remains widely misunderstood.

That "wall" was not designed to banish religion from the public square, as commonly assumed. The phrase appears just once in Jefferson's writings, in a letter to the 1802 Danbury Baptist Association—the context of which is Jefferson's request that they pray for him, and his promise to pray for them in turn. If there's to be "prayer-shaming" in the United States these days then progressivism's favorite Founding Father must be added to the list.[34]

Yet it's exactly this labyrinthine religious legacy that makes Jefferson our best guide out of the troubles of our times—at least for unbelievers of good faith. Deist that he may have been, the sage of Monticello understood that the United States would tear itself apart if religious freedom were not made the "first freedom." He knew from the example of Puritan New England, among other lessons of history, that state-established churches would lead to disaster—exactly because they prohibited *other* people from exercising religious liberty. He could distinguish between what he was free to believe (or not) and what others were free to believe—and he could know simultaneously that his freedom to practice was dependent on theirs and vice versa.

As he famously put it, "The legitimate powers of government extend to such acts only as are injurious to others. But it does me no injury for my neighbor to say there are twenty gods, or no god. It neither picks my pocket nor breaks my leg."[35]

In the end, getting to a more benevolent place depends on a revival of the true Jeffersonians in the United States and elsewhere in the West: reasonable women and men who don't believe that Christians and their perplexing beliefs pick their PayPal accounts or break their legs; who appreciate what the religious do to help the poor and cast-off; and who believe that the ideas of that tribe deserve to be aired without acrimony, whether anyone else is persuaded by anything that's said—or not.

As Sam Harris put it ten years ago, at the end of his *Letter to a Christian Nation*, "The truth is, it really matters what billions of people believe, and why they believe it." The same goes for secularist believers in the kind of faith they're newly building for themselves. The tendency to believe in things beyond our immediate horizons, and to want to universalize that belief, is so self-evidently in need of explanation that several books have lately given it attention from the point of view of evolutionary biology and other scientific perspectives.[36] Secularists want to stand outside that fact-finding and regard themselves as a people set apart, but logic and history aren't on their side.

Now, ten years after Western atheists caught the world's attention by demanding a hearing for their own minority status, the consideration that they asked for—and received—needs to be extended in the opposite direction. Unbelievers and anti-believers should let a new counterculture make its case in the public square: the Christian one. Secularists and progressives might not only challenge themselves to understand where those believers are coming from. They might weigh rather than summarily dismiss the ideas—including some radical ideas—that the believers have been honing during the years of their many routs in the public square, among them that the anti-religious backlash has gone too far; that magnanimity in victory *or* loss is higher ground; that the developing empirical and philosophical critiques of the sexual revolution are legitimate subjects for debate; and that the challenge to the self-understanding of secularists and progressives, according to which secularist progressivism itself is not wholly free of leaps of faith, is also fodder for civil conversation.

Most, and maybe all, of that potential engagement is terra incognita right now. It can't be had without breaking new ground—and breaking ground is work. But the reward might be a more civil place than the one we're all in, if the invitation to that new conversation is not turned down flat.

That is why, in the end, courage is demanded not only of religious believers but of those who disagree with them—the men and women outside their circles whose sense of justice and compassion for the Other is stronger than the temptation to vindictiveness.

Here, too, there may be glimmers of a changing status quo. In 2016, following the death of Justice Antonin Scalia, many people who disagreed with his jurisprudence joined an online hate-in, expressing their contempt and attacking the late justice in rhetorical decibels unimaginable before the instant gratification of cyberspace. Yet one contrarian tweet amid the anger went viral: "Thank you for your service to our country, Justice Scalia. Condolences to your family and friends." It was sent by James Obergefell, the lead plaintiff in *Obergefell v. Hodges*.[37]

To put the point conversely: in widely attended comments delivered in 2014, Elder Dallin H. Oaks of the Church of Jesus Christ of Latter-Day Saints counseled that when religious "positions do not prevail, we should accept unfavorable results graciously and practice civility with our adversaries . . . We should love all people, be good listeners, and show concern for their sincere beliefs. Though we may disagree, we should not be disagreeable. Our stands and communications on controversial topics should not be contentious."[38] This was a sound statement of principle in harmony with an open society, not opposed to it; and it is reasonable to ask that today's Christians be afforded the same courtesy and civility by others.

This, in the end, is what's needed most: for people of truly liberal character to live up to their rhetoric about the diversity of the "human family," and to understand that like any other family, this one includes people who agree to disagree. Courage is required for people like that to stand not only against the cultural tide, but against the inner worms of human nature. As Aleksandr Solzhenitsyn once put it, "every man always has handy a dozen glib little reasons why he is right not to sacrifice himself."[39]

What's needed if we are to change the punitive social and political trajectory of the moment isn't lawsuits from here to eternity. It's two, three, many Nathaniel Saltonstalls—the only judge to have quit the witch trials in Salem. What's needed are people willing to let reason trump pressure and vengeance. In the decades to come, the fate of faithful Western Christians—among them brothers, fathers, mothers, uncles, cousins, grandparents, friends, coworkers, and neighbors—will depend not only on lawyers and courts. It will also hang on whether the people who disagree with them elect to do the right thing by listening to what they have to say, and acknowledging their American right to say it.

Acknowledgments

In 2014, *First Things* magazine invited me to speak in Washington, D.C. on the subject of "The New Intolerance," a talk that became the prolegomenon for this book. Thanks to editor Rusty Reno and others for initiating the reflections.

Thanks also to literary agent Rafe Sagalyn, editor Adam Bellow, and the rest of the HarperCollins team for understanding and encouraging the case made herein.

Aspects of the book's argument have been informed by conversations with friends and colleagues, among them Susan Arellano, Mitchell Boersma, Mary Ellen Bork, Br. Samuel Burke, O.P., Michael Cromartie, Ann and Neil Corkery, Beatriz Delgadillo, Paul Diamond, Sean Fieler, Nathan and Gloria Giesenschlag, Timothy Goeglein, Frank Hanna, Mary Hasson, Russell Hittinger, Fr. Justin Huber, Denise and Andrew Ferguson, Kate and J. D. Flynn, Byron Johnson, Fr. William Joensen, Byron Johnson, Fr. Roger Landry, Allison and Mark Lawrence, Greg Pfundstein, Fr. Arne Panula, Martha and Timothy Reichert, Jonathan Ruano, Fr. Paul Scalia,

Samantha Schroeder, Apoorva Shah, Fr. Alexander Sherbrooke, Gayle and Joel Trotter, George Weigel, Steven White, Fr. Thomas Joseph White, O.P., TJ Whittle, and Andreas Widmer.

I'm grateful for Alex Coblin's eleventh-hour aid, Kathy Medina's cheerful assistance, and the camaraderie of The Kirkpatrick Society. To Gerard V. Bradley and Stanley Kurtz, particular thanks for bringing academic expertise to early versions of the manuscript. As for Kathryn Jean Lopez, Brian Miller, and Christopher White, who improved upon later versions: no earthly reward can suffice.

Thanks above all to my husband Nicholas and to Frederick, Catherine, Isabel, and Alexandra for perpetually re-enchanting the world.

Notes

Introduction:
Among the Believers; or, Why I Wrote This Book

1. Mary Eberstadt, *How the West Really Lost God: A New Theory of Secularization* (West Conshohocken, PA: Templeton Press, 2013).

2. Richard John Neuhaus, *The Naked Public Square: Religion and Democracy in America* (Grand Rapids, MI: Eerdmans, 1984).

3. Sarah Pulliam Bailey, "Houston Subpoenas Pastors' Sermons in Gay Rights Ordinance Case," *Washington Post*, October 15, 2014, https://www.washingtonpost.com/national/religion/houston-subpoenas-pastors-sermons-in-gay-rights-ordinance-case/2014/10/15/9b848ff0-549d-11e4-b86d-184ac281388d_story.html.

4. Julie Bourdon, "InterVarsity Getting Kicked Off College Campuses," Mission Network News, June 11, 2014, https://www.mnnonline.org/news/intervarsity-getting-kicked-college-campuses/.

5. Jason Hanna and Steve Almasy, "Washington High School Coach Placed on Leave for Praying on Field," CNN, October 30, 2015, http://www.cnn.com/2015/10/29/us/washington-football-coach-joe-kennedy-prays/.

6. Chuck Holton, "Military Chaplains the New 'Don't Ask, Don't Tell?,' " CBN News, February 10, 2015, http://www1.cbn.com/cbn news/us/2015/February/Military-Chaplains-the-New-Dont-Ask -Dont-Tell/.

7. Todd Starnes, "Costly Beliefs: State Squeezes Last Penny from Bakers who Defied Lesbian-Wedding Cake Order," FoxNews.com, December 29, 2015, http://www.foxnews.com/opinion/2015/12/29 /bakers-forced-to-pay-more-than-135g-in-lesbian-cake-battle.html.

8. Emily Foxhall, "Attorneys: Katy-Area Teacher Fired for Refusing to Address Girl, 6, as Transgender Boy," Houston Chronicle, November 10, 2015, http://www.chron.com/neighborhood/katy/news /article/Attorneys-Katy-area-teacher-fired-for-refusing-6622339 .php.

9. Samuel Smith, "Evangelical Teacher Fired for Giving Bible to Student Supported by Gov't Commission," Christian Post, January 8, 2015, http://www.christianpost.com/news/evangelical-teacher-fired-for -giving-bible-to-student-supported-by-eeoc-ruling-132293/. The Equal Employment Opportunity Commission later determined that "there is reasonable cause to believe that respondent has discriminated against [the] charging party on the basis of religion and retaliation."

10. Susan Adams, "Mozilla's Brendan Eich: Persecutor or Persecuted?," Forbes, April 4, 2014, http://www.forbes.com/sites/susanadams/2014 /04/04/mozillas-brendan-eich-persecutor-or-persecuted/.

11. Andrew Sullivan, "The Hounding of a Heretic," The Dish blog, April 3, 2014, http://dish.andrewsullivan.com/2014/04/03/the -hounding-of-brendan-eich/.

12. Matthew J. Franck, "Threatened for Her Zeal for the Faith," first things.com, March 13, 2015, http://www.firstthings.com/blogs/first thoughts/2015/03/threatened-for-her-zeal-for-the-faith.

13. Dustin Siggins, "Catholic School Reinstates Teacher Suspended for Defending Catholic Teaching on Facebook," LifeSiteNews, April 10, 2015, https://www.lifesitenews.com/news/catholic-school -reinstates-teacher-suspended-for-defending-catholic-teachin.

14. Adam Liptak, "The Case Against Gay Marriage: Top Law Firms Won't Touch It," *New York Times*, April 11, 2015, http://www.nytimes.com/2015/04/12/us/the-case-against-gay-marriage-top-law-firms-wont-touch-it.html.

15. Matthew J. Franck, "Fired in a Crowded Theater," First Things, October 1, 2010, http://www.firstthings.com/article/2010/10/fired-in-a-crowded-theater.

16. Adam Cassandra, "University of Illinois Says Professor 'Has Not Been Fired' for Teaching Catholic Doctrine on Homosexuality in Catholicism Class—He's Just Not Teaching Classes," cnsnews.com, July 1, 2010, http://www.cnsnews.com/news/article/university-illinois-says-professor-has-not-been-fired-teaching-catholic-doctrine.

17. Natalie Jennings, "Louie Giglio Pulls Out of Inauguration over Anti-Gay Comments," *Washington Post*, January 10, 2013, https://www.washingtonpost.com/news/post-politics/wp/2013/01/10/louie-giglio-pulls-out-of-inaugural-over-anti-gay-comments/.

18. Meghan Duke, "Separation of Pro-Life and State," First Things, January 27, 2010, http://www.firstthings.com/web-exclusives/2010/01/separation-of-prondashlife-and-state.

19. Valerie Richardson, "Gordon College Backlash Sparks Discrimination Accusation," *Washington Times*, April 8, 2015, http://www.washingtontimes.com/news/2015/apr/8/gordon-college-backlash-sparks-discrimination-accu/?page=all.

20. Todd Starnes, "City of Houston Demands Pastors Turn Over Sermons," FoxNews.com, October 14, 2014, http://www.foxnews.com/opinion/2014/10/14/city-houston-demands-pastors-turn-over-sermons.html.

21. As the American Civil Liberties Union explained in a press release of one such suit, for example, "The American Civil Liberties Union will ask a federal court to order the federal government to release documents related to how groups that are awarded government funding contracts are restricting refugee and undocumented immigrant teenagers' access to reproductive health services, including

contraception and abortion." ACLU press release, April 3, 2015, https://www.aclu.org/news/religious-organizations-obstruct-repro ductive-health-care-unaccompanied-immigrant-minors.

22. Peter Hasson, "University of Texas Police Give Preacher Citation for Offending Students," *Daily Caller*, February 10, 2016, daily caller.com/2016/02/10university-of-texas-police-give-preacher -citation-for-offending-students/.

23. Abby Ohlheiser, "Atlanta's Former Fire Chief Sues the City, Says He Was Fired Because of Religious Beliefs," *Washington Post*, February 18, 2015, https://www.washingtonpost.com/news/post-nation /wp/2015/02/18/with-growing-national-support-for-his-cause -atlantas-former-fire-chief-sues-the-city-over-his-dismissal/.

24. Dan Lamothe, "After Court-martial, This Marine Cites Religious Freedom in Her Continued Legal Fight," *Washington Post*, May 21, 2015, https://www.washingtonpost.com/news/checkpoint /wp/2015/05/21/after-court-martial-marine-cites-religious-free dom-in-continued-legal-fight/.

25. Jonathan Petre, "My Ordeal, by Christian Teacher Fired for Offering to Pray for Sick Pupil," *Daily Mail*, December 20, 2009, http://www .dailymail.co.uk/news/article-1237204/Christian-teacher-lost-job -told-praying-sick-girl-bullying.html.

26. Vanessa Allen, "Christian Nurse, 37, Says She Was Sacked for 'Harassment and Bullying' After PRAYING for a Muslim Colleague," *Daily Mail*, January 18, 2015, http://www.dailymail.co.uk/news /article-2915253/Christian-nurse-37-says-sacked-harassment -bullying-praying-Muslim-colleague.html.

27. Richard Scott, "The Foster Parents," chapter 5 in *Christians in the Firing Line* (London: Wilberforce, 2013), pp. 65–81.

28. Scott, "The Van Driver," chapter 2 in ibid., pp. 35–41.

29. Edward Malnick, "Christian Nursery Worker 'Sacked After Refusing to Read Gay Stories to Children,'" *Telegraph*, April 19, 2014, http://www.telegraph.co.uk/news/religion/10776411/Christian -nursery-worker-sacked-after-refusing-to-read-gay-stories-to -children.html.

30. On street preachers jailed in Great Britain, see, for example, Lucinda Borkett-Jones, "Street Preacher Guilty of Using 'Threatening' Language by Quoting Leviticus," *Christian Today*, March 23, 2015, http://www.christiantoday.com/article/street.preacher.guilty .of.using.threatening.language.by.quoting.leviticus/50564.htm. See also Richard Scott, "The Street Preacher," chapter 11 in *Christians in the Firing Line*, which includes other examples, pp. 163–74. Jailed in Canada: In 2008, the Alberta Human Rights Commission charged former Alberta pastor Stephen Boisson with a hate crime for a letter he sent to a local newspaper in 2002 criticizing the teaching of sexuality in the province's education system. See Ethan Cole, "Pastor Acquitted of Hate Crime Charge in Canada," *Christian Post*, December 8, 2009, http://www.christianpost.com/news/pastor-acquitted -of-hate-crime-charge-in-canada-42190/.

31. Howell Davies, "Uproar in Oxford as Trinity Hosts Christian Group with Controversial Views on Homosexuality," *Independent*, March 26, 2013, http://www.independent.co.uk/student/news /uproar-in-oxford-as-trinity-hosts-christian-group-with-contro versial-views-on-homosexuality-8550531.html.

32. John L. Allen, *The Global War on Christians: Dispatches from the Front Lines of Anti-Christian Persecution* (New York: Image Books, 2013), p. 4.

33. Tom Batchelor, "Christians Almost Completely Destroyed by ISIS Fanatics in Syria, Archbishop of Aleppo," *Express*, October 21, 2015, http://www.express.co.uk/news/world/613514/Islamic-State-Chris tians-Syria-wiped-out-jihadi-militants.

34. Nina Shea, "The Islamic State's Christian and Yizidi Sex Slaves," *American Interest*, July 31, 2015, http://www.the-american-inter est.com/2015/07/31/the-islamic-states-christian-and-yizidi-sex -slaves/.

35. Sarah Kaplan, "Has the World 'Looked the Other Way' While Christians Are Killed'?" *Washington Post*, April 7, 2015, https://www .washingtonpost.com/news/morning-mix/wp/2015/04/07/has-the -world-looked-the-other-way-while-christians-are-killed/.

36. Allen, ibid., p. 19.

37. Abraham Cooper and Yitzchok Adlerstein, "Mideast Christians Deserve U.S. Refuge," *Wall Street Journal*, December 17, 2015. http://www
.wsj.com/articles/mideast-christians-deserve-u-s-refuge-1450396991.

38. "Lord Carey: Britain Has a Duty to Rescue Syrian Refugees," *Telegraph*, September 5, 2015.

39. John Hall, "Pope Francis Condemns the Pursuit of Money as 'the Dung of the Devil' and Decries the 'Genocide' of Christians in the Middle East as a 'Third World War,' dailymail.co.uk, July 10, 2015. http://www.dailymail.co.uk/news/article-3156055/Pope-Francis
-condemns-pursuit-money-dung-devil-decries-genocide-Christians
-Middle-East-World-War.html.

40. Jack Moore, "European Parliament Recognizes ISIS Killing of Religious Minorities as Genocide," *Newsweek*, February 4, 2016, http://
www.newsweek.com/european-parliament-recognizes-isis-killing
-religious-minorities-genocide-423008.

41. Nina Shea, "For Christians and Yazidis Fleeing Genocide, the Obama Administration Has No Room at the Inn," nationalreview.com, September 22, 2015, http://www.nationalreview.com/article/424401
/christians-yazidis-persecuted-iraq-syria-refugees-excluded.

42. Daniel Williams, "Open the Door for Persecuted Iraqi Christians," *Washington Post*, December 4, 2015, https://www.washingtonpost
.com/opinions/open-the-door-for-persecuted-iraqi-christians
/2015/12/04/51db87c0-9969-11e5-8917-653b65c809eb_story.html.

43. Alasdair MacIntyre, *After Virtue: A Study in Moral Theory*, 2nd ed. (Notre Dame, IN: University of Notre Dame Press, 1984), p. 263. The often-quoted last paragraph is an object of considerable discussion among religious traditionalists, particularly via writer Rod Dreher at *The American Conservative* magazine and his blog at theamericanconservative.com. That closing passage reads in part: "What matters at this stage is the construction of local forms of community within which civility and the intellectual and moral life can be sustained through the new dark ages which are already upon us. And if the tradition of the virtues was able to survive the horrors

of the last dark ages, we are not entirely without grounds for hope. This time however the barbarians are not waiting beyond the frontiers; they have already been governing us for quite some time. And it is our lack of consciousness of this that constitutes part of our predicament. We are waiting not for a Godot, but for another—doubtless very different—St. Benedict."

44. Matthew Spence, "I was a Closeted Christian in the Pentagon," *Washington Post*, April 10, 2016. https://www.washingtonpost.com /opinions/i-was-a-closeted-christian-at-the-pentagon/2016/04 /08/0eea5468-dbd2-11e5-81ae-7491b9b9e7df_story.html.

45. Kathryn Jean Lopez, "A Pentecostal, A Southern Baptist, and a Catholic Walked into the Press Club," *nationalreview.com*, July 2, 2013, http://www.nationalreview.com/corner/352595/pentecostal -southern-baptist-and-catholic-walked-press-club-kathryn-jean-lopez.

46. Michael Sean Winters, "J'ACCUSE! Why Obama Is Wrong on the HHS Conscience Regulations," *National Catholic Reporter*, January 21, 2012. http://ncronline.org/blogs/distinctly-catholic/jaccuse -why-obama-wrong-hhs-conscience-regulations.

47. He added, "His successor will pick up the shards of a ruined society and slowly help rebuild civilization, as the church has done so often in human history." See Tim Drake, "Cardinal George: The Myth and Reality of 'I'll Die in My Bed,'" *National Catholic Register*, April 17, 2015, http://www.ncregister.com/blog/tim-drake/the-myth-and-the -reality-of-ill-die-in-my-bed.

48. Billy Graham, "Prepare for Persecution," *Decision*, November 2015, http://billygraham.org/decision-magazine/november-2015/prepare -for-persecution-a-message-from-billy-graham/.

49. R. Albert Mohler, Jr., *We Cannot Be Silent: Speaking Truth to a Culture Redefining Sex, Marriage, and the Very Meaning of Right and Wrong* (Nashville, TN: Thomas Nelson, 2015), p. 135.

50. Christian Deguit, "Pope Francis: Christians Being 'Politely Persecuted' Under Guise of 'Modernity and Progress,'" *Christian Daily*, April 15, 2016.

51. Rosa Parks, with Jim Haskins, *My Story* (New York: Dial Books, 1992).

52. Randy Boyagoda, *Richard John Neuhaus: A Life in the Public Square* (New York: Image Books, 2015), pp. 104–111.

53. Daniel K. Williams, *Defenders of the Unborn: The Pro-Life Movement before Roe v. Wade* (New York: Oxford University Press, 2016).

54. See, for example, Drake Bennett, "What Happened to the Anti-Porn Feminists?," boston.com, March 6, 2005, http://www.boston.com /news/globe/ideas/articles/2005/03/06/x_ed_out?pg=full.

55. Christopher Lasch, *The Minimal Self: Psychic Survival in Troubled Times*, paperback ed. (New York: Norton, 1986), p. 259.

1: The Roots of the New Intolerance

1. Robert Royal, *The Catholic Martyrs of the Twentieth Century: A Comprehensive World History* (New York: Crossroad, 2006).

2. Jenna Portnoy, "Bill Would Let Parents 'Opt Out' on Literature," *Washington Post*, February 26, 2016, https://www.washingtonpost .com/local/virginia-politics/in-virginia-classrooms-should-parents -block-sexually-explicit-literature/2016/02/25/fa5aa396-db67-11e5 -81ae-7491b9b9e7df_story.html.

3. For an analysis of *Wolf Hall*, see George Weigel, "'Wolf Hall' and Upmarket Anti-Catholicism," firstthings.com, April 22, 2015, http://www.firstthings.com/web-exclusives/2015/04/wolf-hall-and -upmarket-anti-catholicism.

4. Eberstadt, ibid., pp. 78-81.

5. Richard Dawkins, *The God Delusion* (Boston and New York: Houghton Mifflin, 2006), p. 37.

6. Sam Harris, *Letter to a Christian Nation* (New York: Knopf, 2006), pp. vii–ix.

7. Kevin Phillips, *American Theocracy: The Peril and Politics of Radical Religion, Oil, and Borrowed Money in the 21st Century* (New York: Viking, 2006), quotes on pp. xiv and xv.

8. Damon Linker, *The Theocons: Secular America Under Siege* (New York: Doubleday, 2006), pp. 4 and 14.

9. Will Herberg, *Protestant-Catholic-Jew: An Essay in American Religious Sociology* (Chicago: University of Chicago Press, 1983), pp. 46–47.

10. E-mail communication with George Weigel, April 3, 2016.

11. Speech by President Obama, April 6, 2008, YouTube, https://www.youtube.com/watch?v=DTxXUufI3jA.

12. Jordan Fabian, "Obama Concerned by 'Less-than-Loving' Christians," *The Hill*, April 7, 2015, http://thehill.com/blogs/blog-briefing-room/news/238064-obama-concerned-by-less-than-loving-christians.

13. "President Obama & Marilynne Robinson: A Conversation in Iowa," *New York Review of Books*, November 5, 2015, http://www.nybooks.com/articles/2015/11/05/president-obama-marilynne-robinson-conversation/.

14. Hillary Clinton, keynote address at the 2015 Women in the World Summit, http://www.hillaryhq.com/2015/05/women-in-world-summit-2015-keynote.html.

15. Philip Elliott, "Joe Biden Pushes New LGBT Protections, Calls 2016 GOP Candidates 'Homophobes,'" *Time*, October 3, 2015, http://time.com/4060530/joe-biden-republican-gay-rights-homophobes/.

16. *Romer v. Evans*, 517 U.S. 620 (1996).

17. Pew Research Center, "America's Changing Religious Landscape: Christians Decline Sharply as Share of Population; Unaffiliated and other Faiths Continue to Grow," May 12, 2015, http://www.pewforum.org/2015/05/12/americas-changing-religious-landscape/.

18. See Eberstadt, *How the West Really Lost God*, pp. 122–24.

19. See Andrew Ferguson, "Revenge of the Sociologists: The Perils of Politically Incorrect Academic Research," *Weekly Standard*, July 30, 2012, http://www.weeklystandard.com/revenge-of-the-sociologists/article/648829.

20. "Christian British Airways Employee Sent Home for Wearing Cross Loses Appeal over Religious Discrimination," *Daily Mail*, February 12, 2010, http://www.dailymail.co.uk/news/article-1250459/Christian-British-Airways-employee-sent-home-wearing-cross

-loses-appeal-religious-discrimination.html. In 2013, the European Court of Human Rights found in favor of the plaintiff and ordered the United Kingdom to pay damages and costs. Ian Johnston, "Christian Airline Worker Can Wear Cross, Europe Court Says," NBCNews.com, January 15, 2013, http://worldnews.nbcnews.com /_news/2013/01/15/16522912-christian-airline-worker-can-wear -cross-europe-court-says.

21. Emily Cummins, "New Jersey Teacher Fired after Giving Student a Bible to Teach Again after Government Ruling," NJ.com, January 7, 2015, http://www.nj.com/warrenreporter/index.ssf/2015/01 /bible_teacher_new_jersey_eeoc.html.

22. Karl Popper, *The Open Society and its Enemies* (Princeton, NJ: Princeton University Press, 2013). First published Routledge 1945.

2: Anatomy of a Secularist Witch Hunt

1. Christina Larner, "Witchcraft Past and Present," in *Witchcraft and Religion* (New York: Blackwell, 1984), p. 88.

2. See, for example, Philip Terzian, "Remember McMartin," *Weekly Standard*, November 11, 2011, http://www.weeklystandard.com /remember-mcmartin/article/607988, and Clyde Haberman, "The Trial That Unleashed Hysteria Over Child Abuse," *New York Times*, March 9, 2014, http://www.nytimes.com/2014/03/10/us/the-trial -that-unleashed-hysteria-over-child-abuse.html?_r=0.

3. Maura Casey, "How the Daycare Child Abuse Hysteria of the 1980s Became a Witch Hunt," *Washington Post*, July 31, 2015, https://www.washingtonpost.com/opinions/a-modern-witch-hunt /2015/07/31/057effd8-2f1a-11e5-8353-1215475949f4_story.html.

4. See Dorothy Rabinowitz, *No Crueler Tyrannies: Accusation, False Witness, and Other Terrors of Our Times* (New York: Free Press, 2003).

5. Stacy Schiff, *The Witches: Salem, 1692* (Boston: Little, Brown, 2015), p. 9.

6. Miller's popular account of the similarities between Salem village in the late 1600s and the so-called Red Scare of the mid-twentieth century is obviously an imperfect albeit interesting analogy. For starters, we do not know how many accused witches in Massachusetts *thought* of themselves as witches—whereas we do know that some accused communists in fact knew themselves to be communists. See Whittaker Chambers, *Witness* (New York: Random House, 1952).

7. For a contrarian view of the revolution's legacy, see Mary Eberstadt, *Adam and Eve after the Pill: Paradoxes of the Sexual Revolution* (San Francisco: Ignatius Press, 2012).

8. Hanna Rosin, "The Dirty Little Secret: Most Gay Couples Aren't Monogamous," *Slate*, June 26, 2013, http://www.slate.com/blogs /xx_factor/2013/06/26/most_gay_couples_aren_t_monogamous _will_straight_couples_go_monogamish.html.

9. See, for example, Peter Singer, "Heavy Petting," nerve.com, March 12, 2001, http://www.utilitarian.net/singer/by/2001—.htm. For discussion, see also William Saletan, "Shag the Dog," *Slate*, April 5, 2001, http://www.slate.com/articles/news_and_politics/frame_game /2001/04/shag_the_dog.html.

10. Alexa Tsoulis-Reay, "What It's Like to Date a Horse," *New York*, November 20, 2014, http://nymag.com/scienceofus/2014/11/what-its -like-to-date-a-horse.html#.

11. C. Everett Koop, "Why Defend Partial-Birth Abortion?," *New York Times*, September 26, 1996, http://www.nytimes.com/1996/09/26 /opinion/why-defend-partial-birth-abortion.html.

12. Kenneth Silverman, *The Life and Times of Cotton Mather* (New York: Harper & Row, 1984), p. 115.

13. Ibid., p. 425.

14. See "Freedom to Marry, Freedom to Dissent: Why We Must Have Both: A Public Statement," *RealClearPolitics*, April 22, 2014, http:// www.realclearpolitics.com/articles/2014/04/22/freedom_to_marry _freedom_to_dissent_why_we_must_have_both_122376.html.

15. Schiff, *The Witches*, pp. 209–10.

16. Brian Hutchinson, "'God Bless' Is Very Offensive to Me": 'Viking with a Ph.D.' in Rant After Christian's Job Application," *National Post*, October 8, 2014, http://news.nationalpost.com/news/canada/b-c-woman-says-she-was-rejected-for-job-because-shes-christian-as-company-manager-says-her-religion-offends-norse-culture. He also explained: "The Norse background of most of the guys at the management level means that we are not a Christian organization, and most of us actually see Christianity as having destroyed our culture, tradition and way of life."

17. "Trinity Western Law School Accreditation Denial Upheld by Ontario Court," CBCNews, July 2, 2015, http://www.cbc.ca/news/canada/british-columbia/trinity-western-law-school-accreditation-denial-upheld-by-ontario-court-1.3136529. This decision was later overturned by a British Columbia Supreme Court judge. See "Trinity Western Law School Decision Overturned by Supreme Court," CBCNews, December 10, 2015, http://www.cbc.ca/news/canada/british-columbia/trinity-western-law-society-bc-supreme-court-1.3359942.

18. Jonathan Petre, "Christian Minister Disciplined by Prison Authorities for Quoting Verses from the Bible Deemed to Be Homophobic," dailymail.co.uk, October 31, 2015. http://www.dailymail.co.uk/news/article-3298454/A-Christian-minister-disciplined-prison-authorities-quoting-verses-Bible-deemed-homophobic.html.

19. Among other such cases cited in this book, one particularly interesting example is that of a preacher who was hauled into jail and accused of homophobia for a twenty-minute public sermon. As his recording of the talk bore out, he had in fact not even mentioned homosexuality. http://www.dailymail.co.uk/news/article-3099487/Christian-preacher-arrested-held-cell-11-HOURS-lesbian-falsely-accuses-homophobia.html. According to the story, he subsequently "received £2,500 and a contribution toward his legal fees for wrongful arrest, false imprisonment and breach of his human rights in an out-of-court settlement."

20. John Bingham, "Preacher Accuses Judge of 'Redacting' the Bible," *Telegraph*, March 30, 2015, http://www.telegraph.co.uk/news /religion/11505466/Preacher-accuses-judge-of-redacting-the-Bible .html.

21. Christopher Hitchens, "Unanswerable Prayers," *Vanity Fair*, September 2, 2010. http://www.vanityfair.com/culture/2010/10/hitchens -201010.

22. Emma Green, "Prayer Shaming after a Mass Shooting in San Bernardino," theatlantic.com, December 2, 2015. http://www.theatlantic .com/politics/archive/2015/12/prayer-gun-control-mass-shooting -san-bernardino/418563/.

23. Patrick Foster, "God Banished from Downton Abbey, Says Show's Historical Advisor," *The Telegraph*, November 15, 2015, http://www .telegraph.co.uk/news/media/11997169/God-banished-from -Downton-Abbey-says-shows-historical-advisor.html.

24. Melissa Barnhart, "College Student Denied Admission into Program Because He Said God Is Most Important in His Life," *Christian Post*, April 25, 2014, http://www.christianpost.com/news/college -student-denied-admission-into-program-because-he-said-god-is -most-important-in-his-life-118531/.

25. Anita Singh, "Hilary Mantel: Catholic Church Is Not for Respectable People," *The Telegraph*, May 13, 2012, http://www.telegraph.co.uk /culture/9262955/Hilary-Mantel-Catholic-Church-is-not-for -respectable-people.html.

26. Michael E. Price, "Human Herding: How People Are Like Guppies," *Psychology Today*, June 25, 2013, https://www.psychologytoday .com/blog/darwin-eternity/201306/human-herding-how-people -are-guppies.

27. Russell Goldman, "Here's a List of 58 Gender Options for Facebook Users," *abcnews.com*, February 13, 2014. http://abcnews.go.com /blogs/headlines/2014/02/heres-a-list-of-58-gender-options-for -facebook-users/.

28. Sarah Griffiths, "Facebook's New Gender Options Launch in the U.K.: Users Can Now Select One of 70 Choices Including

'Asexual' and 'Two-Spirit,' " dailymail.co.uk, June 27, 2014. http://
www.dailymail.co.uk/sciencetech/article-2672359/Facebooks
-new-gender-options-launch-UK-Users-select-one-70-choices
-including-asexual-two-spirit.html.

29. Michelle Boorstein, "Facebook Wouldn't Let a Catholic Priest Use
the Title 'Father.' Now He's Fighting Back," *Washington Post*, August 27, 2015. https://www.washingtonpost.com/news/acts-of-faith
/wp/2015/08/27/facebook-wouldnt-let-a-catholic-priest-use-the
-title-father-now-hes-fighting-back/.

30. H. R. Trevor-Roper, *The European Witch-Craze of the Sixteenth and
Seventeenth Centuries and Other Essays* (New York: Harper Torch-
books, 1969), p. 127.

31. Dave Huber, "Hillary Clinton Gets 91% of Harvard Faculty Donations," College Fix, February 10, 2016, http://www.thecollegefix
.com/post/26185/.

32. "Vicious Spies and Killers Under the Mask of Academic Physicians,"
Pravda, January 13, 1953, http://www.cyberrussr.com/rus/vrach
-ubijca-e.html.

33. Trevor-Roper, *The European Witch-Craze*, p. 166.

34. Kirsten Powers, *The Silencing: How the Left Is Killing Free Speech*
(Washington, DC: Regnery, 2015), p. 53.

35. J. D. Flynn, "The One and Only Culture War: A Reply to David
Brooks," *First Things*, September 18, 2015.

36. Yanan Wang, "Feminist Germaine Greer Still Pummeled for Mi-
sogynistic Views Toward Transwomen," *Washington Post*, November 3, 2015, https://www.washingtonpost.com/news/morning-mix
/wp/2015/11/03/feminist-germaine-greer-still-being-pummelled
-for-misogynistic-views-toward-transwomen/.

37. Peter Tatchell, "Twitter Mob Who Vowed to Kill Me Have It All
Wrong," *International Business Times*, February 17, 2015, http://www
.ibtimes.co.uk/peter-tatchell-twitter-mob-who-vowed-kill-me
-over-mary-beard-transgender-letter-have-it-all-wrong-1488351.

38. Elizabeth Nolan Brown, "LGBT Rights vs. Religious Freedom Looms
Large at #AtlanticLGBT Summit," Reason.com, December 12,

2015, https://reason.com/blog/2015/12/12/atlantic-lgbt-summit
-dispatches.

39. Dahlia Lithwick, "Chilling Effect: How the Attacks on a University of
Virginia Law Professor Are Bad for Academia, and All of Us," *Slate*,
May 28, 2014, http://www.slate.com/articles/news_and_politics
/jurisprudence/2014/05/douglas_laycock_gets_smeared_lgbtq
_groups_attack_on_the_university_of_virginia.html.

40. Remarks by the President at National Prayer Breakfast, Washington Hilton, Washington, D.C., February 6, 2014, https://www
.whitehouse.gov/the-press-office/2014/02/06/remarks-president
-national-prayer-breakfast.

3: Acclaiming Diversity vs. Hounding the Heretics

1. For more on InterVarsity, see https://intervarsity.org. See also
Kimberly Winston, "InterVarsity, College Christian Group,
'De-Recognized' at California State University Campuses," *Huffington Post*, September 9, 2014, http://www.huffingtonpost.com/2014
/09/09/intervarsity-sanctioned-california-state-university_n
_5791906.html.

2. Brooke Metz, "Cal State Retracts Recognition for InterVarsity on
all 23 Campuses," *USA Today*, September 18, 2014, http://college
.usatoday.com/2014/09/18/cal-state-retracts-recognition-for-inter
varsity-on-all-23-campuses/.

3. Samuel Smith, " 'Attending College Should Not Cost Me My
Faith,' Says Chi Alpha President Whose Chapter Lost Official
Status on Campus for Requiring Leaders to Be Christian," *Christian Post*, March 31, 2013, http://www.christianpost.com/news
/attending-college-should-not-cost-me-my-faith-says-chi-alpha
-president-whose-calif-chapter-lost-official-status-on-campus-for
-requiring-leaders-to-be-christian-136687/.

4. Carole J. Williams, "Supreme Court Rules Against UC Student Group
that Excluded Gays," *Los Angeles Times*, June 29, 2010, http://articles
.latimes.com/2010/jun/29/nation/la-na-court-christians-20100629.

5. Adam Liptak, "Justices Rule Against Group That Excludes Gay Students," *New York Times*, June 28, 2010, http://www.nytimes .com/2010/06/29/us/29court.html?_r=0.

6. Jess Bravin and Nathan Koppel, "School Can Deny Funding to Group," *Wall Street Journal*, June 29, 2010.

7. Christian Legal Society Chapter of University of California, *Hastings College of Law v. Martinez*, 561 U.S. 661 (2010).

8. "In 'CLS v. Martinez' Ruling, Sharply Divided Supreme Court Undermines Freedom of Association on Campus," June 28, 2010, Foundation for Individual Rights in Education, press release, https://www.thefire.org/in-cls-v-martinez-ruling-sharply-divided -supreme-court-undermines-freedom-of-association-on-campus/.

9. Suzanne Garment and Leslie Lenkowsky, "Supreme Court's Ruling in College Case Strikes Blow to Charities," *Chronicle of Philanthropy*, June 30, 2010, https://philanthropy.com/article/Supreme-Court-s -Ruling/160407.

10. James Tonkowich, *The Liberty Threat: The Attack on Religious Freedom in America Today* (Charlotte, NC: St. Benedict Press, 2014), pp. 81–82.

11. "Christians Criticise Christian Union Ban," *Christian Today*, November 21, 2006, http://www.christiantoday.com/article/christians .criticise.christian.union.ban/8419.htm.

12. "Exeter Christian Union Threatens Legal Action over 'Ban,'" *Guardian*, November 17, 2006, http://www.theguardian.com/edu cation/2006/nov/17/highereducation.students.

13. Tonkowich, *The Liberty Threat*, pp. 80–81.

14. Julie R. Posselt, *Inside Graduate Admissions: Merit, Diversity, and Faculty Gatekeeping* (Cambridge, MA: Harvard University Press, 2016).

15. Scott Jaschik, "Inside Graduate Admissions," *Inside Higher Ed*, January 6, 2016, https://www.insidehighered.com/news/2016/01/06 /new-book-reveals-how-elite-phd-admissions-committees-review -candidates.

16. David French, "Want Intellectual Diversity in Higher Education? Start with Ending Anti-Christian Discrimination," *nationalreview*

.com, January 7, 2016, French's story has a happier ending: "To their credit, the committee members apologized and offered him admission." http://www.nationalreview.com/corner/429414/stop -anti-christian-discrimination-higher-education.

17. Private communication from someone present at the meeting, February 2016.

18. Rod Dreher, "Grad School: No Christians Need Apply," *American Conservative*, January 6, 2016, http://www.theamericanconservative .com/dreher/grad-school-no-christians-need-apply/.

19. See, for example, Chris Weller, "There's a New Path to Harvard and It's Not in a Classroom," *Tech Insider*, September 3, 2015, http://www .techinsider.io/homeschooling-is-the-new-path-to-harvard-2015-9.

20. Dana Goldstein, "Liberals, Don't Homeschool Your Kids: Why Teaching Children at Home Violates Progressive Values," *Slate*, February 16, 2012, http://www.slate.com/articles/double_x/doublex /2012/02/homeschooling_and_unschooling_among_liberals_and _progressives_.html.

21. Jeffrey Tayler, "The Religious Have Gone Insane: The Separation of Church and State—and Scalia from His Mind," *Salon*, July 26, 2015, http://www.salon.com/2015/07/26/the_religious_have_gone_insane _the_separation_of_church_and_state_and_scalia_from_his_mind/.

22. See, for example, Richard Dawkins, "Childhood, Abuse, and the Escape from Religion" chapter 9 in *The God Delusion* (Boston: Houghton Mifflin Harcourt, 2006).

23. Amanda Marcotte, "Texas Governor Appoints a Homeschooler to Head State Education Board," *Slate*, June 26, 2015, http://www.slate .com/blogs/xx_factor/2015/06/26/donna_bahorich_is_a_home schooler_why_is_she_going_to_head_the_state_school.html.

24. Catherine J. Ross, "Fundamentalist Challenges to Core Democratic Values: Exit and Homeschooling," *William & Mary Bill of Rights Journal* 18, no. 4 (2010), http://scholarship.law.wm.edu/cgi/view content.cgi?article=1160&context=wmborj.

25. Peter Hitchens, *The Rage Against God: How Atheism Led Me to Faith* (Grand Rapids, MI: Zondervan, 2010), p. 204.

26. Hitchens, ibid., p. 207.

27. *2014-2015 NEA Resolutions*, http://www.nea.org/assets/docs/nea -resolutions-2014-15.pdf, p. 38.

28. "Home-Schoolers Incensed by Drill Scenario," *Muskegon Chronicle*, September 22, 2004, via link at http://www.freerepublic.com/focus /f-news/1223565/posts?page=105.

29. David Levinsky, "Hostage Drill Prepares School for Crisis," *Burlington County Times*, April 2, 2007, http://www.debatepolicy.com /showthread.php?2184-Hostage-drill-prepares-school-for-crisis.

30. Robert H. Bork, *Slouching Towards Gomorrah: Modern Liberalism and American Decline* (New York: HarperCollins, 1996), p. 291.

31. Walt Tutka, "New Jersey Teacher Fired after Giving Student a Bible to Teach Again after Government Ruling," NJ.com, January 7, 2015, http://www.nj.com/warrenreporter/index.ssf/2015/01/bible _teacher_new_jersey_eeoc.html.

32. "2014–2015 NEA Resolutions," National Education Association, http://www.nea.org/assets/docs/nea-resolutions-2014-15.pdf.

33. Evan Allen, "Gordon College Leader Joins Request for Exemption to Hiring Rule," *Boston Globe*, July 4, 2014, https://www.bostonglobe .com/metro/2014/07/03/gordon-college-president-signs-letter -asking-for-religious-exemption-from-order-banning-anti-gay-dis crimination/79cgrbFOuUg7lxH2rKXOgO/story.html.

34. David French, "The Persecution of Gordon College," *National Review*, January 26, 2015, http://www.nationalreview.com/article /397677/persecution-gordon-college-david-french.

35. Ibid.

36. Robert A. J. Gagnon, "Gordon College Wins—and Loses," First Things, May 5, 2015. Gagnon http://www.firstthings.com/web -exclusives/2015/05/gordon-college-winsand-loses.

37. Tina McCormick, "Gordon College Prevailed, But Will the Country?," *New Boston Post*, December 8, 2015. http://newbostonpost .com/2015/12/08/gordon-college-prevailed-but-will-the-country/.

38. Curtis Fraser, "EC [Emmanuel College] Athletics to End Relationship with Gordon College over Letter," *Hub*, February 25, 2015,

http://ecthehub.com/2015/02/25/ec-athletics-to-end-relationship -with-gordon-college-over-letter/.

39. Oliver Ortega, "Lynn Public Schools Sever Relationship with Gordon College," *Boston Globe*, August 30, 2014, https://www.bostonglobe .com/metro/2014/08/29/lynn-public-schools-sever-relationship -with-gordon-college/aw1KwO4RGVpn284rR1jTgO/story.html.

40. Valerie Richardson, "Gordon College Backlash Sparks Discrimination Accusations Against Gay Advocates," *Washington Times*, April 8, 2015, http://www.washingtontimes.com/news/2015/apr/8 /gordon-college-backlash-sparks-discrimination-accu/?page=all.

41. Stanley Kurtz reported extensively on the King's College case in the *National Review* online. See Stanley Kurtz, "Long Live King's," nationalreview.com, April 5, 2005. http://www.nationalreview.com /article/214083/long-live-kings-stanley-kurtz.

42. Ibid.

43. See Scott Jaschik, "Church and State," *Inside Higher Ed*, April 6, 2005, https://www.insidehighered.com/news/2005/04/06/kings.

44. Peter Wood, "The Old College Try," *American Conservative*, May 8, 2006, http://www.theamericanconservative.com/articles/the-old -college-try/.

45. Peter Conn, "The Great Accreditation Farce," *Chronicle of Higher Education*, June 30, 2014, http://chronicle.com/article/The-Great -Accreditation-Farce/147425/.

46. Nick Corasaniti, "Bernie Sanders Makes Rare Appeal to Evangelicals at Liberty University," *New York Times*, September 14, 2015. http://www.nytimes.com/politics/first-draft/2015/09/14/bernie -sanders-makes-rare-appeal-to-evangelicals-at-liberty-university/.

47. Kirsten Powers, *The Silencing: How the Left Is Killing Free Speech* (Washington, DC: Regnery, 2015), p. 65.

48. Samantha Vincent, "Christian Convert, Former Lesbian Draws Protesters for Upcoming Lecture at TU [University of Tulsa]," *Tulsa World*, November 12, 2015, http://www.tulsaworld.com/news/local /christian-convert-former-lesbian-draws-protesters-for-upcoming -lecture-at/article_fbec9164-65cc-5528-ab31-5e809719a70b.html.

49. Austin Yack, "Rowdy Protestors Disrupt Talk in Support of Traditional Marriage at UCSB," *College Fix*, May 27, 2015, http://www.thecollegefix.com/post/22613/.

50. Hemant Mehta, "This Is a Powerful Way to Combat a Christian Speaker at Your University," Patheos, February 17, 2014, http://www.patheos.com/blogs/friendlyatheist/2014/02/17/this-is-a-powerful-way-to-combat-a-christian-speaker-at-your-university/.

51. Howell Davies, "Uproar in Oxford as Trinity Hosts Christian Group with Controversial Views on Homosexuality," *Independent*, March 26, 2013, http://www.independent.co.uk/student/news/uproar-in-oxford-as-trinity-hosts-christian-group-with-controversial-views-on-homosexuality-8550531.html.

4: Civil Rights Talk vs. McCarthyite Muscle

1. Carol Cratting, "25-Year Sentence in Family Research Council Shooting," CNN.com, September 19, 2013, http://www.cnn.com/2013/09/19/justice/dc-family-research-council-shooting/.

2. Jessica Valenti, "Violent Anti-Choice Rhetoric Must End, or Anti-Abortion Violence Never Will," *The Guardian*, November 29, 2015. http://www.theguardian.com/commentisfree/2015/nov/29/planned-parenthood-colorado-springs-shooting-no-more-baby-parts.

3. Petula Dvorak, "Words Matter in Attacks on Planned Parenthood, Black Lives Matter, and Muslim Refugees," *Washington Post*, November 30, 2015. https://www.washingtonpost.com/local/words-matter-in-attacks-on-planned-parenthood-black-lives-matter-and-muslim-refugees/2015/11/30/ce568abc-9765-11e5-b499-76cbec161973_story.html.

4. Michelle Goldberg, "The Link Between Anti-Abortion Rhetoric and the Planned Parenthood Attack," *Slate*, November 30, 2015. http://www.slate.com/articles/double_x/doublex/2015/11/planned_parenthood_attack_and_anti_abortion_rhetoric_the_undeniable_connection.html.

5. For examples of "Right Wing Watch's" enemies lists, see http://www
.rightwingwatch.org/category/people.

6. See https://www.splcenter.org/fighting-hate/extremist-files.

7. " 'Religious Liberty' and the Anti-LGBT Right," Southern Poverty
Law Center, February 11, 2016. https://www.splcenter.org/20160211
/religious-liberty-and-anti-lgbt-right.

8. See, for example, http://www.hrc.org/blog/10-shocking-facts-about
-the-alliance-defending-freedom.

9. Martin Finucane, "ACLU To Represent NAMBLA," *Washington
Post*, August 31, 2000. http://www.washingtonpost.com/wp-srv/ap
online/20000831/aponline171914_000.htm.

10. When the legal organization Liberty Counsel took on the case of
Kim Davis, the Kentucky clerk fired for refusing to issue marriage
licenses to same-sex couples, numerous organizations and com-
mentators decried the legal organization as a "hate group." See,
for example, http://www.rightwingwatch.org/content/meet-hate
-group-trying-turn-kim-davis-anti-gay-rosa-parks.

11. Teresa Stanton Collett post in "Symposium: Ensuring Abortion
Safety in a Declining Market for Abortion Services," SCOTUSblog,
January 7, 2016, http://www.scotusblog.com/2016/01/symposium
-ensuring-abortion-safety-in-a-declining-market-for-abortion
-services/. For her argument about the use of ultrasound, see also
http://sblog.s3.amazonaws.com/wp-content/uploads/2013/06
/27817-pdf-Brown-II-final-petition.pdf.

12. https://www.facebook.com/naralprochoiceamerica/videos/1015
3692832059321/.

13. http://actnow.prochoiceamerica.org/sign/151022_full-collett
/&utm_source=FB&utm_medium=CKCollett?#.VpkRMzZh2i4.

14. Email communication with Teresa Collett, January 15, 2016.

15. Ryan T. Anderson, *Truth Overruled: The Future of Marriage and Religious Freedom* (Washington, D.C.: Regnery Publishing, 2015). See also
Ryan T. Anderson, Robert P. George, and Sherif Gergis, *What Is Marriage? Man and Woman: A Defense* (New York: Encounter Books, 2012.

16. See, for example, Joanna Rothkopf, "Ed Schultz Flips Out On Indiana Anti-Gay Law Supporter, Cuts His Mic," *Salon*, April 2, 2015. The piece includes a video of the exchange. http://www.salon.com /2015/04/02/ed_schultz_yells_at_rfra_supporter_then_cuts_his_mic/.

17. http://dailysignal.com/2014/07/31/new-york-times-reporter-peo ple-deserving-incivility/ and http://dailysignal.com/2014/07/29 /exchange-two-new-york-times-writers-marriage-equality-civility/].

18. Robert Barnes, "The Right Finds A Fresh Voice On Same-Sex Marriage," *Washington Post*, April 15, 2015. https://www.washingtonpost .com/politics/courts_law/a-fresh-face-emerges-as-a-leader-in-the -movement-against-same-sex-marriage/2015/04/15/d78cf256 -dece-11e4-be40-566e2653afe5_story.html.

19. Kelsey Harkness, "K-12 School Removes Washington Post Profile of Ryan T. Anderson from its Facebook Page. Here's Why." *Daily Signal*, April 17, 2015. http://dailysignal.com/2015/04/17/k-12-school -removes-washington-post-profile-of-ryan-t-anderson-from-its -facebook-page-heres-why/.

20. http://www.royalgazette.com/article/20151125/NEWS/151129791.

21. Lucy Sherriff, "Oxford Abortion Debate Cancelled Due to 'Security Concerns' Over Planned Protest," *Huffington Post United Kingdom*, November 18, 2014, http://www.huffingtonpost.co.uk/2014/11/18 /oxford-abortion-debate-cancelled-security-concerns_n_6176846 .html.

22. "Stanford Students Demand Tax on Free Speech Be Removed," Stanford Anscombe Society press release, March 19, 2014, http:// www.stanfordanscombe.org/march-19-2014.html. See also Kylie Jue, "University Provides Security Funding for 'Anti-LGBT' Conference," *Stanford Daily*, March 28, 2014, http://www.stanforddaily. com/2014/03/28/university-provides-security-funding-for-anti -lgbt-conference/.

23. Foundation on Individual Rights in Education, "Spotlight on Speech Codes 2016: The State of Free Speech on Our Nation's Campuses," https://www.thefire.org/spotlight-on-speech-codes-2016/.

24. Cristina Odone, "The New Intolerance: Will We Regret Pushing Christians Out of Public Life?," *New Statesman*, January 14, 2014, http://www.newstatesman.com/2014/01/new-intolerance-will-we -regret-pushing-christians-out-public-life.

25. Isaac Chotiner, "No, Atheist Intolerance Is Not Destroying Western Society," *New Republic*, January 19, 2014, https://newrepublic .com/article/116150/atheist-intolerance-not-dominating-western -society.

5: Inquisitors vs. Good Works

1. Louis Jacobson, "Does the Catholic Church Provide Half of Social Services in the U.S.?," PolitiFact, March 19, 2013, http://www.politi fact.com/truth-o-meter/statements/2013/mar/19/frank-keating /does-catholic-church-provide-half-social-services-/. While disputing the claim that the church is responsible for fully half of U.S. social services, PolitiFact concluded nonetheless that "Catholic groups are among the biggest providers of social-service charity in the nation."

2. Michael Levenson, "Workers Rush to Fill Void Left by Boston Agency's Decision," *Boston Globe*, March 11, 2006, http://www.boston .com/news/local/articles/2006/03/11/workers_rush_to_fill_void_ left_by_boston_agencys_decision/.

3. Archbishop Joseph E. Kurtz, President, Address to the United States Conference of Catholic Bishops, November 16, 2015, http://www .usccb.org/about/leadership/usccb-general-assembly/2015-novem ber-meeting/usccb-general-assembly-2015-november-presidential -address.cfm.

4. Archbishop Charles J. Chaput, "The Joy of the Gospel and the Gospel of Life," *First Things*, August 30, 2015.

5. John Ashmen, "Freedom to Care for the Poor," Real Clear Religion, November 10, 2015, http://www.realclearreligion.org/articles /2015/11/10/freedom_to_care_for_the_poor.html.

6. Arthur C. Brooks, *Who Really Cares: The Surprising Truth About Compassionate Conservatism* (New York: Basic Books, 2006), p. 10.

7. Ibid., p. 35.

8. Ibid., p. 36.

9. Ibid., p. 5.

10. Remarks by the President at National Prayer Breakfast, February 6, 2014. https://www.whitehouse.gov/the-press-office/2014/02/06/remarks-president-national-prayer-breakfast.

11. Terence P. Jeffrey, "Obama Touts Religious Liberty to Pope While Litigating to Force 15 Dioceses to Cooperate in Abortion," CNSNews.com, September 23, 2015, http://www.cnsnews.com/news/article/terence-p-jeffrey/obama-touts-religious-liberty-pope-while-litigating-force-15-dioceses.

12. For updated lists of those lawsuits, see the Becket Fund for Religious Liberty's "HHS Information" page, http://www.becketfund.org/hhsinformationcentral/.

13. Sarah Pulliam Bailey and Abby Ohlheiser, "Pope Francis Meets with Little Sisters of the Poor, Nuns Involved in an Obamacare Lawsuit," *Washington Post*, September 23, 2015, https://www.washingtonpost.com/news/acts-of-faith/wp/2015/09/23/pope-francis-meets-with-little-sisters-of-the-poor-nuns-involved-in-an-obamacare-lawsuit/.

14. "ACLU Announces Lawsuit Against Catholic Hospital System for Failing to Provide Emergency Medical Care to Pregnant Women," press release, American Civil Liberties Union, October 1, 2015, https://www.aclu.org/news/aclu-announces-lawsuit-against-catholic-hospital-system-failing-provide-emergency-medical-care.

15. "ACLU Files Lawsuit to Investigate Scope of the Problem and Government's Role in Denying Care," press release, American Civil Liberties Union, April 3, 2015, https://www.aclu.org/news/religious-organizations-obstruct-reproductive-health-care-unaccompanied-immigrant-minors.

16. For more about the scope of the USCCB's involvement with refugees, see for example "Unlocking Human Dignity: A Plan to Transform

the U.S. Immigrant Detention System: A Joint Report of Migration and Refugee Services/United States Conference of Catholic Bishops and the Center for Migration Studies," 2015, http://www.usccb.org /about/migration-and-refugee-services/upload/unlocking-human -dignity-report.pdf.

17. John L. Allen Jr., "Pope Francis Criticizes Gay Marriage, Backs Ban on Contraception," Crux, January 16, 2015, http://www.cruxnow .com/church/2015/01/16/pope-francis-criticizes-gay-marriage -backs-contraception-ban/.

18. "Religious Groups Push U.S. to Take In 100,000 Syrian Refugees," Religion News Service, September 9, 2015, http://www.religionnews .com/2015/09/09/religious-church-syrian-refugees/.

19. For an account of how NARAL's targeting of pregnancy centers looks from the other side, see Ben Johnson, "LifeSiteNews Uncovers NARAL's 7-Point Plan to Destroy Crisis Pregnancy Centers," *LifeSite-News*, January 13, 2015, https://www.lifesitenews.com/opinion /lifesitenews-uncovers-narals-7-point-plan-to-destroy-crisis-preg nancy-cente.

20. Alexei Koseff, "Battle over Abortion Rights in California Shifts to Cri-sis Pregnancy Centers," *Sacramento Bee*, December 6, 2015, http:// www.sacbee.com/news/politics-government/capitol-alert/article 48338410.html.

21. Wesley J. Smith, "Belgian Catholic Nursing Home Sued for Refus-ing Euthanasia," *nationalreview.com*, January 10, 2016, http://www .nationalreview.com/corner/429528/belgian-catholic-nursing -home-sued-refusing-euthansia.

22. Wesley J. Smith, "What Euthanasia Enthusiasts Really Want," *First Things*, January 8, 2016, http://www.firstthings.com/web-exclusives /2016/01/what-euthanasia-enthusiasts-really-want.

23. Steve Doughty, "Catholic Adoption Agency Loses Five Year Legal Battle over Its Refusal to Accept Gay Couples," *Daily Mail*, November 2, 2012, http://www.dailymail.co.uk/news/article-2226829/Catholic -Care-Adoption-agency-loses-5-year-legal-battle-refusal-accept -gay-couples.html.

24. Katherine Weber, "Second School Drops Out of 'Operation Christmas Child' Following Atheist Lawsuit, Parents Vow to Raise Money on their Own," *Christian Post*, November 21, 2013. http://www.christianpost.com/news/second-school-drops-out-of-operation-christmas-child-following-atheist-lawsuit-parents-vow-to-raise-money-on-their-own-109196/.
25. Ibid.
26. Ibid.
27. Ashley Samelson McGuire, "Why Freedom of Worship Is Not Enough," *First Things*, February 22, 2010, http://www.firstthings.com/web-exclusives/2010/02/why-ldquofreedom-of-worshiprdquo-is-not-enough.
28. Jonathan Rauch, "The Emerging Gay Majority," *Advocate*, December 2010, http://www.jonathanrauch.com/jrauch_articles/the-emerging-gay-majority.

6: What Is to Be Done; or, How to End a Witch Hunt

1. Margaret Eby, "HGTV Cancels 'Flip It Forward' over Hosts David and Jason Benham's Controversial Anti-Gay, Anti-Choice Views," *Daily News* (New York), May 8, 2014, http://www.nydailynews.com/entertainment/tv/hgtv-cancels-flip-hosts-controversial-views-article-1.1784687.
2. Lisa de Moraes, "Brothers Yanked by HGTV Respond: If Our Faith Costs Us a TV Show, So Be It," *Deadline Hollywood*, May 8, 2014, http://deadline.com/2014/05/url-benham-brothers-respond-hgtv-cancelled-show-726663/.
3. David Levin, ed., *What Happened in Salem: Documents Pertaining to the Seventeenth-Century Witchcraft Trials,* 2d ed. 1960 (New York: HBJ College & School Division), pp. 125–26.
4. As Elizabeth Anscombe, one of the most notable philosophers of the twentieth century, as well as a practicing Catholic, observed in a famous essay called "Contraception and Chastity": "There always

used to be a colossal strain in ancient times; between heathen morality and Christian morality, and one of the things pagan converts had to be told about the way they were entering on was that they must abstain from fornication. This peculiarity of the Christian life was taught in a precept issued by the Council of Jerusalem, the very first council of the Christian Church." Collected in Janet E. Smith, ed., *Why* Humanae Vitae *Was Right: A Reader* (San Francisco: Ignatius Press, 1993), pp. 119–45.

5. W. Bradford Wilcox and Robert I. Lerman, *For Richer, for Poorer: How Family Structures Economic Success in America* (Washington, DC: American Enterprise Institute, 2014), https://www.aei.org/publication/for-richer-for-poorer-how-family-structures-economic-success-in-america/.

6. Ashley Samelson, "Lipstick Jungle," *Wall Street Journal*, September 26, 2008. http://www.wsj.com/articles/SB122238618931577035.

7. Christopher Beach, "Tragedy on College Campuses," FRC Blog, May 4, 2010, http://www.frcblog.com/2010/05/tragedy-on-college-campuses/.

8. Damon Linker, "Love and Sex in the Age of Tinder," *The Week*, August 12, 2015, http://theweek.com/articles/571317/love-sex-age-tinder.

9. "Abortion, Infanticide, and Allowing Babies to Die, Forty Years On," *Journal of Medical Ethics* 39, no. 5 (May 2013), http://jme.bmj.com/content/39/5.toc.

10. Wesley J. Smith, "Infanticide Now 'Debatable' in Bioethics," nationalreview.com, December 15, 2014, http://www.nationalreview.com/human-exceptionalism/394684/infanticide-now-debatable-bioethics-wesley-j-smith.

11. Walter Lippmann, *A Preface to Morals* (New York: Macmillan 1929), p. 291.

12. See his book *The American Sex Revolution* (Boston: Porter Sargent, 1956).

13. Michel Houellebecq, *The Elementary Particles* (New York: Knopf, 2000), p. 94.

14. Martin Amis, *The Pregnant Widow* (New York: Deckle Edge, 2010), p. 307.

15. Christopher White, "Surrogates and Their Discontents," *Public Discourse*, August 16, 2012, http://www.thepublicdiscourse.com/2012/08/6137/.

16. Paul Farrell, "Baby Gammy, born into Thai surrogacy scandal, granted Australian citizenship," *theguardian.com*, Jan. 19, 2015. http://www.theguardian.com/australia-news/2015/jan/20/baby-gammy-born-into-thai-surrogacy-scandal-granted-australian-citizenship.

17. Christopher White, "Surrogacy Gives Birth to an Unusual Alliance," *Wall Street Journal*, September 4, 2014. http://www.wsj.com/articles/christopher-white-surrogacy-gives-birth-to-an-unusual-alliance-1409872645.

18. Russell D. Moore, *Onward: Engaging the Culture Without Losing the Gospel* (Nashville, TN: B&H Books, 2015), p. 184.

19. Robert P. George, "What is Religious Freedom?," *Public Discourse*, July 24, 2013, http://www.thepublicdiscourse.com/2013/07/10622/.

20. See, for example, Mary Eberstadt, "The New Intolerance," *First Things*, March 2015. http://www.firstthings.com/article/2015/03/the-new-intolerance.

21. See George Weigel's discussion of Weiler's thesis in *The Cube and the Cathedral: Europe, America, and Politics Without God* (New York: Basic Books, 2005), especially pp. 64–98.

22. George Yancey and David A. Williamson, *So Many Christians, So Few Lions: Is There Christianophobia in the United States?* (Lanham, MD: Rowman & Littlefield, 2015).

23. Terry Eagleton, *Reason, Faith, and Revolution: Reflections on the God Debate* (New Haven, CT: Yale University Press, 2009), p. 33.

24. David Bohon, "Air Force Suspends 'Christian Just War Theory' for Missile Officers," *New American*, August 16, 2011, http://www.the

newamerican.com/culture/faith-and-morals/item/976-air-force
-suspends-christian-just-war-theory-class-for-missile-officers.

25. By way of introduction, see the entry on "Just War Theory" in the peer-reviewed Internet Encyclopedia of Philosophy, http://www .iep.utm.edu/justwar/.

26. Robert Royal, *A Deeper Vision: The Catholic Intellectual Tradition in the Twentieth Century* (San Francisco: Ignatius Press, 2015).

27. Joseph Bottum, *An Anxious Age: The Post-Protestant Ethic and the Spirit of America* (New York: Image, 2014), p. 153.

28. Weigel, *The Cube and the Cathedral*, p. 148.

29. Kevin Seamus Hasson, *The Right to Be Wrong: Ending the Culture War over Religion in America* (New York: Image, 2015), p. 148.

30. For an examination of how this point played out in the historical example of the English Reformation, see historian Eamon Duffy, *The Stripping of the Altars: Traditional Religion in England 1400–1580.* (New Haven, CT: Yale University Press, 1992).

31. Tonkowich, *The Liberty Threat*, p. 5.

32. Michael Novak, "The Faith of the Founding," *First Things*, April 2003, http://www.firstthings.com/article/2003/04/the-faith-of-the -founding. See also his book *On Two Wings: Humble Faith and Common Sense at the American Founding* (New York: Encounter Books, 2001).

33. Mark A. Beliles and Jerry Newcombe, *Doubting Thomas? The Religious Life and Legacy of Thomas Jefferson* (New York: Morgan James Publishing, 2015).

34. Emma Green, "Prayer Shaming after a Mass Shooting in San Bernardino," *Atlantic*, December 2, 2015, http://www.theatlantic.com /politics/archive/2015/12/prayer-gun-control-mass-shooting-san -bernardino/418563/.

35. Thomas Jefferson, *Notes on the State of Virginia*, Query XVII, 1781– 1783, https://www.monticello.org/site/research-and-collections /jeffersons-religious-beliefs.

36. See, for example, Dean H. Hamer, *The God Gene: How Faith is Hardwired into Our Genes* (New York: Doubleday, 2004); and Matthew

Alper, *The "God" Part of the Brain: A Scientific Interpretation of Human Spirituality and God* (Naperville, IL: Sourcebooks, 2006). See also Andrew Newberg and Mark Robert Waldman, *How God Changes Your Brain: Breakthrough Findings from a Leading Neuroscientist* (New York: Ballantine Books, 2009).

37. Trudy Ring, "Jim Obergefell's Gracious Tweet on Antonin Scalia's Death," *advocate.com*, February 4, 2016. http://www.advocate.com /marriage-equality/2016/2/14/jim-obergefells-gracious-tweet -antonin-scalias-death.

38. Lisa Riley Roche, "Calls for Civility Accompany Same-Sex Marriage Action," *Deseret News*, October 6, 2014. http://www.deseretnews .com/article/865612533/Calls-for-civility-accompany-same-sex -marriage-action.html?pg=all.

39. Aleksandr I. Solzhenitsyn, *The Gulag Archipelago* (1974; reprint New York: HarperCollins, 2007), p. 17.

About the Author

MARY EBERSTADT is an essayist and author of several influential books, including *How the West Really Lost God*, *Adam and Eve After the Pill*, and *Home-Alone America*. She is also the editor of *Why I Turned Right*. Her novel *The Loser Letters* has recently been adapted for the stage. Eberstadt is a frequent contributor to *Time*, the *Wall Street Journal*, the *National Review*, the *Weekly Standard*, and *First Things*. She lives in the Washington, D.C., area.